Secrets of Religion

A Temporary Separation of God and Religion

By
Mike Bhangu

BBP
Copyright 2014

Https://www.facebook.com/pages/Author-Mike-Bhangu/130968380378729

ISBN 978-0-9866602-2-1 (pbk.).--ISBN 978-0-9866602-3-8 (ebook)

Library and Archives Canada Cataloguing in Publication

Bhangu, Mike Singh, author
   Secrets of religion: a temporary separation of God and religion
   / Mike Bhangu.

Issued in print and electronic formats.
ISBN 978-0-9866602-2-1 (pbk.).--ISBN 978-0-9866602-3-8 (ebook)

1. Religion. 2. Religions. 3. God. I. Title.

BL80.3.B53 2014   **201**   **C2014-907706-8**
                                     C2014-907707-6

Illustrator: Mike Singh Bhangu
Published by BB Productions
Merritt, B.C., Canada
crpublications@gmail.com

Dedicated to the God seeker.

Table of Contents

Preface
Introduction

Chapter 1

Part I: Age of Darkness

Part II: Canon Reloaded

Table of Contents

Table of Contents

Preface

Who is right and who is wrong? Is death the end or is death another experience? What about life and the Universe; a Darwinized fluke or a divine design?

I feel like a newborn piece of asteroid debris blasting into emptiness. Something went *"bang"* and pushed me into nothingness, and when I thought all was lost and the end was at hand, it pulled me back in again. Something pulled me back in again and temporarily crushed my ego into oblivion. The silencing of my ego allowed my mind to travel to places it had never been. There, discover I did the secrets of religion, and the answers to the above questions.

A factual and philosophical commentary, the articles within this manuscript were written individually while on the journey to discover The Great Architect. Subsequently, they were brought together to present some of my findings, and after reading through the book, I'm hoping specific ideas become evident.

1. Religions were infiltrated by eco-political attitudes.

2. A selfish agenda misleads and misled the general public.

3. Religions accommodate doctrine that wrongly divides people.

4. The commonalities between religions are an indication of a higher purpose.

5. Popular culture doesn't harness the human being's potential.

6. And the most purposeful life values an individual can facilitate. That is, if a person would like a good existence after the body perishes.

Secrets of Religion strives to take you closer to the heavens. To that end, the illusions that are religion and popular culture hinder spiritual progression.

Please, keep in mind that I do not challenge people or God, but instead, ideas. Try not to take my thoughts personal, and if there are any mistakes, accept my apology.

X

Introduction

Religions and popular culture have matured to bury one-half of the human condition, the human spirit. That was done for power, control, secular ambition, consumerism, and economics.

To know something, the information of that something must be absorbed. For example, a person will only come to know mathematics if he or she is exposed to the principles of math. But if mathematical information is difficult to access, the likelihood of a person absorbing it to know it will be extremely low.

Like Mr. Hyde, popular culture has attached little value to the knowledge that nurtures the human spirit. Evidence of that is the lack of knowledge required to know the spirit. Rarely is the idea of God, the spiritual realm, or life after death discussed by the popular media or during the water-cooler conversation.

Instead, our popular culture teaches that life is a fluke, death is the end, and all that matters is consumption of the secular and the senses.

Our popular culture, through the many communication mediums, gives little attention to the invisible within the human fortress. Simultaneously, it distracts the mind from searching for it. What's more, those entrusted with the knowledge of the spirit, religions, are guilty of riddles and political spin--as you'll discover within the pages of this manuscript.

Religions and popular culture have confused the individual and the person is trained to unknowingly ignore the metaphysical. The popular culture hides the invisible realm to prop-up consumerism and economics, and religions hoard metaphysical truths and manipulate doctrine for control, power, and secular ambitions. Left standing in this whirlwind is the person. Today, our spirit is in need of reclamation.

The world can be divided into two, the rulers and the ruled. Each division is governed by different values. The ruled are fed beliefs that maintain the status of the rulers, and placed in a built environment that facilitates this. In that environment, popular culture and religions are tools of the rulers used to force-feed the ruled values. In their delivery of those beliefs, in the case of religions, Godly doctrine was used to gift-wrap the deception. The challenge of the God seeker is to see beyond the artificial illusion created by the misdirection.

1

When reality is observed through the eyes of the ruled and through the eyes of the ruler, the structure of society and the popular beliefs fostered by it, all make sense, in particular, the elements that do not benefit the person.

Divided into three chapters, *Secrets of Religion* takes the first step toward truly understanding the metaphysical self and the invisible realm, by revealing religions and popular culture for what they've evolved to become.

Chapter One will attempt to lift the veil that religions have placed over political motivations, and Chapter One will address doctrine that doesn't feel completely truthful. Chapter Two will attempt to reveal the manner in which popular culture works to assassinate the spirit. And Chapter Three shadows the idea of love. All chapters simultaneously strive to reveal some of the prevalent commonalities among religions.

The first chapter is sectioned into three parts.

Chapter1.1: Age of Darkness, with a focus on the three most affluent religions--Christianity, Judaism, and Islam, presents rational answers to such questions as:

- Why were plausible lies inserted into religious doctrine?
- What elements are anti-god or untruthful?
- Why do religions war and what are the doctrinal inspirations?
- Why do religions stand on opposite ends even though they all carry a common message?
- How is dogma twisted?
- Who are God's children?

Chapter 1.2: Canon Reloaded, struggles with concerns such as:

- Who wrote the Holy Books?
- How can an individual choose Heaven?
- What is the God image?
- What is sin, and without a religion, how can a person be forgiven?
- Why do civilizations end?

This section further presents several other very important concepts.

- The location of The Supreme Consciousness.
- The common goal of most prayers of most religions.
- Hell and the Devil but with a more reasonable explanation.
- Easter Eggs and Jesus.
- The power of the Word.
- The nature of God's Spirit.
- The universal principle of Karma.

Chapter 1.3: Sikhie and Hinduism, travels away from the Abrahamic religions to review such ideas as seers, mystics, gods, goddesses, an appearance, and rituals.

Chapter 2: Angels and Demons, builds on the first chapter and efforts to present several very important concepts.

- How to discover a unique life purpose.
- The attributes of a God Consciousness.
- The Darwin deception.
- The characteristics of the angelic and the demonic.
- The soul.
- The root of sin and from where wickedness truly stems.
- The importance of the beautiful half of the mind's condition.
- This thing called the consumer culture and the manner in which it restricts spiritual progress.

Chapter 3: Love, unveils an unbreakable induction.

Secrets of Religion presents ideas that are sure to turn several of the concepts within the goblet that is religion upside down. But rest assured; the ideas are eventually placed right side up--less the politically motivated doctrine, of course.

There are two volumes to *Secrets of Religion.* This is Volume 1; meant to prepare the reader for the second volume, by relieving the obstacles that are religion and popular culture. The second volume details such notions as the meditation techniques that activate a person's inner energy, specific resonances and their potential to offer nirvana, the experience that is heaven, the pineal gland, the nature of miracles, and so on. Volume 2 will take the God seeker to the next level.

3

This manuscript stands on the premise that the person is built to be, built to be a patron of peace, a scholar of kindness, and an instrument of truth.

Chapter 1
Part I: Age of Darkness

The Betrayed

Religions have behaved corruptly and that's led many reasonable people to walk away from religion. However, as they turned their back, they unwittingly walked away from The Great Architect. Unable to distinguish between religion and The Formless, before examining the other religious doctrines to possibly fill-in the blanks created by the corruption, they claim that the entirety of religions are out-to-lunch and this idea of God must also be a false construct.

Betrayal has inspired many persons to the cave of the agnostic. Some managed to crawl back out and others are still stuck in the darkness. Until a Divine intervention or thoughts reach an absolute conclusion, the cave will remain a truth within the mind of the betrayed.

To provide the first is not in my power, but with the second, I think I can help. Thoughts at a near-end tend to interpret the corruption as separate from the heavens, and the division provides a much more reasonable perspective. Religious practices and doctrine examined after the partition have the potential to reveal The Great Architect. The opening to this chapter provides ample examples of the betrayal, and I'm hoping those examples will frame the religious ethos that might not be truthful.

Chasing Angels

I've unknowingly spent most of my life digging through religious riddles hidden underneath political truths. I've unknowingly spent most of my life shifting through the truths of religion and the truths of the Universe. And I've unknowingly spent most of my life, deaf and blind, chasing angels.

I've unknowingly spent because pieces of popular religions don't really make rational sense. For some reason, they create a divide between us, and us and the heavens. For instance, they readily hide the fact that there is truth in other religions. For some reason, they support ideas that pit the likes of Jesus against the likes of Jesus. The thousands of Christian denominations are prime illustrations. And for some reason, they allowed self-interest to attribute untruths to the mouths of the God sent. For example, the Catholic Church tricked the masses to crusade by blurring the idea of salvation and sanctioning the act of murder in the name of Jesus.[1], and the Islamic kingdoms of the past, such as the Ottoman Empire, used their faith to justify the slavery of other humans. The non-Muslims they didn't enslave were considered second-class citizens, as revealed by Robert Spencer in his book, *The Politically Incorrect Guide to Islam and the Crusades* (Regnery Publishing, 2005), page 54.

But perhaps, I'm mistaken, and God truly did inspire the many divisions between religions, the many denominations within, and the many chains and bloodstained weapons. Maybe, I'm mistaken, and God truly did inspire evil things like the Catholic crusades,[2] the spiritual decimation of the First Nations,[3] the Spanish Inquisition,[4] Euro-centric motivations,[5] the attack on the Americans, the oppression of the Palestinians, slavery, doomsday predictions, and forceful conversions.

The Islamic Empire of the Mughals was the most infamous for such a practice. According to author, Max Arthur McAuliffe, in his book, *The Sikh Religion: Volume I*, the Mughals ruthlessly murdered hundreds of thousands in their attempt to convert others to Islam. According to Sikh history and the stories found within Sikh literature, in their attempt to convert others to Islam, the Mughals employed heinous and ungodly measures. For example, they bricked alive two infant children on their refusal to accept the supremacy of Islam (the two youngest sons of Guru Gobind Singh), they executed two of India's greatest holy men because they were non-Muslim (**Guru Arjan** and **Guru Tegh Bahadur**), and they hunted all who belonged to the noble House of

8

Nanak simply because they belonged to the House of Nanak. Nanak is the founder of Sikhism. The Sikh religion is given more attention in section three of this chapter. (I suppose this is a good time to mention that the words in bold are defined at the back of the book, in the glossary).

The Afghan Muslims behaved just as barbarically. They murdered en masse so to deny religious alternatives. In the year 1762, during one of their invasions into India, they annihilated twenty-thousand innocent Sikh women and children. They did horrible things such as throwing children into the air and spearing them as they fell, and snatching infants from their mothers, cutting them into pieces, and giving the remains back. The Afghan Muslims targeted women and children in an effort to deny the future of the Sikh faith.

History of the Origin and Progress of the Sikhs, written in 1778 by James Browne, tells that when the Afghan Muslims didn't murder, they would enslave non-Muslims--in particular, women. The women were typically sold into the sex trade or given to the soldiers.

John Malcolm, in his book, *Sketch of the Sikhs*, published in 1812, describes an instance when the Afghanies actually used the blood of slaughtered Sikhs to wash the walls of mosques. The Afghanies believed that the Sikhs had polluted the mosques by entering them and the blood bath was meant to purify the buildings.

Again, I could be wrong and God is truly concerned with control, power, and secular ambitions. Who knows, perhaps only some of us are God's children? God knows, that's exactly the message all popular religions seem to give and condition their followers into believing. For example, the most affluent religions of the world, Judaism, Christianity, and Islam, each claim that their doctrine is the only acceptable to God and no others. They also push the propaganda that, after the body falls, God will punish those who are not a member of their religion. Jack Nelson-Pallmeyer, an expert on the topic, writes:

> *"Jews claim to be God's chosen people, recipients of land, special promises, and noble mission. Christians say Jesus fulfilled Hebrew scriptural promises--a claim denied by Jews--that Jesus is the only way to God. The Quran is Allah's divinely inspired corrective to the errors propagated through the texts and conduct*

9

of Jews and Christians. It is the religious duty of Muslims to struggle (jihad) against unbelievers in order to establish a world in accord with Allah's intent."[6]

Not surprisingly, these three have made trouble and killed each other for centuries in the name of the One God's Will.

What to make of all this, who is right and who is wrong? Could it be that they all hold truth? Could it be that they all harbour some degree of falsehood? And what explains the anti-God behaviour?

After taking the time to examine religions, it becomes apparent that they were infiltrated by selfish ambitions. What else explains the evil perpetrated under the banner of the Cross, the Star, and Islam? I've come to understand the pieces of doctrine that advocate or glorify murder, that depict God as violent, that use fear to gain obedience, that divide humanity, or that claim only a specific people are Godly as economic and political injections. Insertions designed by rulers to incite people to conquer others, to expand the boundaries of a nation or empire, to inspire and justify the brutish behaviour that always accompanies expansion, or to maintain the current state of affairs.

Framed by the above stipulations, there appear to be religious ideas that are not inspired by The Great Architect, and they've led to ungodly activities. The forthcoming pages provide several examples of that type of canon, and their design was inspired by the elite demographic to maintain and enhance their power, and of course, to control the behaviour of the bewildered herd.

This doesn't imply that political ambitions led to the establishment of religions. Most religions came before the politics and selfish people and groups eventually hijacked them. They astutely recognized religion as an instrument able to impress their will and increase their wealth. In addition, religion left to its own devices could threaten the power of those who rule, a lesson the early Christians taught the Roman Empire. When a religion does begin to pose a threat to the establishment, the threatened will penetrate it and steer it away from them. In most cases, most religions came into existence as a challenge to the status quo, and by their nature, they were a threat to those who ruled.

Cunningly, after the incursion by selfish ambitions, ungodly doctrine strategically found its way among canon that emanates the aroma of Godliness.

10

Godless dogma was placed among the Godly so to give the appearance of a divine inspiration, and to manipulate the follower into believing it. Heavenly concepts are a part of all popular religion and they typically stress love, truth, compassion, humility, selflessness, unity, etc.

Celestial concepts are bundled with the opposite, and innocently, some people haven't thought enough about the origins and the history of religion to understand some of the politics. Like those played by the Islamic Empires and the Roman Emperor Constantine.

Constantine decided to mix Pagan ideas from the Mithra tradition with Christian ideas, and unfortunately, some of the flock can't see the difference between the holy and the manmade--for example, they openly idolize the bones of dead saints.

Scholars suggest that Constantine, when he was attempting to convert the Roman Empire from a Pagan Empire to a Christian Kingdom, behaved more as a politician than a Christian. Constantine allowed Pagan ideas such as idolizing bones to continue to exist so to appease the Pagan population. The symbol of the cross with a circle is another example of the marriage (it actually represents the Pagan Sun god), the idea of Trinity existed before Jesus but with different characters, and the Vatican is built on ancient Pagan spiritual land. Constantine's manipulation of the Christian dogma is given more attention in an impending article.

The same kind of political agenda is evident in Islam, and it would seem that Godly ideas sit among doctrine that feels not so celestial. In the case of Islam, violent and oppressive passages were the outcome and nation building was the motivation. The atrocities committed by past Islamic Empires are the evidence.

> *"(Remember) when your Lord inspired the angels, 'Verily, I am with you, so keep firm those who have believed. I will cast terror into the hearts of those who have disbelieved, so strike them over the necks, and smite over all their fingers and toes.'"--*(Qur'an 8:12)

> *"And when the sacred months have passed, then kill the polytheists wherever you find them and capture them and besiege*

them and sit in wait for them at every place of ambush. But if they should repent, establish prayer, and give zakah, let them [go] on their way. Indeed, Allah is Forgiving and Merciful."--(Qur'an 9:5)

After searching the Islamic doctrine, it became clear that violence is sanctioned. It's also obvious that the Muslim Empires would not have become so large if not for the sword and a hand to hold it--if not for doctrine that rationalizes the brutality of conquest. Or, for that matter, slave labour. The *Qur'an* makes several references to the subjugated.

"And marry those among you who are single and those who are fit among your male slaves and your female slaves..."--(Qur'an 24:32)

"And if any of your slaves ask for a deed in writing (to enable them to earn their freedom for a certain sum), give them such a deed if you know any good in them; yes, give them something yourselves out of the means which Allah has given to you."--(Qur'an 24:33)

Although Islam permits slavery, the *Qur'an* also suggests that it is righteous to free a slave.

"Righteousness is not that you turn your faces toward the east or the west, but [true] righteousness is [in] one who believes in Allah, the Last Day, the angels, the Book, and the prophets and gives wealth, in spite of love for it, to relatives, orphans, the needy, the traveler, those who ask [for help], and for freeing slaves..."--(Qur'an 2:177)

A contradiction is evident. To have slaves is acceptable, but to free a slave is true righteousness. This is a prime example of the mix between Godly and ungodly canon.

The Prophet Mohammad existed and a celestial spark inspired his thoughts. After his birth, the world became a better place, as it did after the birth of people like Moses, Zoroaster, Buddha, Nanak, and Jesus. But as you'll discover in an upcoming article, Mohammad didn't write or compile the

Qur'an. The creation of the *Qur'an* came after Mohammad ascended into "The White Light". Perhaps, if the *Qur'an* was finalized under his supervision, passages that create conflict and inspire slavery would not exist.

Islam isn't the only that accommodates the idea of oppressing another. Along with a superiority complex, as detailed in the upcoming articles, the Jewish doctrine too permits slavery.

> *"When Israel grew strong, they put the Canaanites to forced labor, but did not drive them out completely."*--(Judges 1:28)

> *"However, you may purchase male and female slaves from among the nations around you. You may also purchase the children of temporary residents who live among you, including those who have been born in your land. You may treat them as your property, passing them on to your children as a permanent inheritance. You may treat them as slaves, but you must never treat your fellow Israelites this way."*--(Leviticus 25:44–46)

And the Jewish doctrine also condemns the act. A contradiction there is.

> *"Whoever steals a man and sells him, and anyone found in possession of him, shall be put to death."*--(Exodus 21:16)

The inconsistencies exist because Godly ideas are presented with ideas not so Godly. The mix is the outcome of political and economic motivations. In the case of slavery, free labour is much more profitable than paying someone.

However, some people don't bother to question, and maybe, they're scared of the unknown and the mysterious muzzles their curiosity for reason. More important, no matter the scattered punctures, under the umbrella held by religion, it does feel safe and with purpose. The illusion can be enough to get through the everyday motions. But like every other, that artificial apparition will also fade and along with it the feelings it gives. One day, the circumstances will push us into the rain to search for God again.

I apologize if you find the ideas I'm presenting offensive. But please don't be mistaken. To temporarily sever the conditioned associations religions have instilled is not to separate the holy from the heavens. Nor is it a challenge aimed in that direction. It's an attempt to discover God again and to bring that truth back to every religion.

Assuming God exists.

The excerpts from the different Holy Texts are all translations, and none of them were initially written in the English language. Misinterpretations and mistranslations are plausible.

14

God's People

> *"...It identifies the Israelites as God's chosen people, who, depending on which passages are cited, are destined by God either to be the vehicle through which God blesses all the nations, or to dominate the nations of the world. Most common are passages that confirm the latter view, with Isaiah's words being representative: Your gates shall always be open; day and night they shall not be shut, so that nations shall bring you their wealth, with their kings led in procession. For the nation and kingdom that will not serve you shall perish; those nations shall be utterly laid to waste. (60:11-12)"*--(Jack Nelson-Pallmeyer, *Is Religion Killing Us?: violence in the Bible and the Quran*, 2005, pg. 32)

The Jewish institution claims that they are the chosen people of God and no others. I think that idea was taught to the Jewish people to give them hope, confidence, self-respect, status, and strength to endure the hardship. From the philosopher's stone that I'm leaning on, all are the people of God and not just a specific group. To claim that one is more than another is to suggest that one is more than human.

The early history of the Jewish people is marked by hardship. They were persecuted and enslaved by the Babylonians, the Egyptians, the Greeks, and the Romans. Consequentially, the Jewish collective intelligence adopted a slave's mindset.

To break that mindset, it's plausible that the Jews were taught to believe they were God's people. A people can endure so much more when they believe that they're the chosen ones and their hardship has meaning. So much more can be achieved than through the mind of a slave.

It's also very possible that the Jewish people were given that notion so to persuade them to nation-build and to take another people's territory. The history of the Jewish institution, as depicted by the *Old Testament*, is extremely violent and on many occasions Biblical characters murdered and stole in God's Will, and in the end, to nation-build, because they believed they were God's chosen people.

The Jewish institution is not alone in their claim that only they are the people of God. Islam also asserts the same.

*"Truly, the religion with God is Islam."--(*Qur'an 3:19)

Moreover, the institution of Islam labels all non-Muslims as infidels (nonbelievers), and they view the non-Muslim as lesser because of their non-Islamic values.

To give weight to that claim, elements of their doctrine suggest that it is the Will of God to subject the people of the world to Islamic rule. Maybe, that's why the Islamic institution was so deeply involved in the slave trade and able to morally justify caging other human beings like animals. Maybe, that's why the Islamic Empires, lost to the history books, readily murdered non-Muslims and took what was theirs.

> *"According to the founder and 'supreme guide' of the Muslim Brotherhood, Sheikh Hasan al-Banna, 'It is the nature of Islam to dominate, not to be dominated, to impose its law on all nations and to extend its power to the entire planet"* (quoted in Taheri, 1987).[7]

> Ayatollah Ruhollah Khomeini once said, *"Moslems have no alternative... to an armed holy war against profane governments....Holy war means the conquest of all non-Moslem territories....It will...be the duty of every able bodied adult male to volunteer for this war of conquest, the final aim of which is to put Koranic law in power from one end of the earth to the other."*[8]

> *"And fight them until there is no more Fitnah (disbelief) and the religion will all be for Allah Alone."*--(Qur'an 8:39)

> *"Fight against those who believe not in Allah, nor in the Last Day, nor forbid that which has been forbidden by Allah and His Messenger and those who acknowledge not the religion of truth (i.e. Islam) among the people of the Scripture (Jews and Christians), until they pay the Jizyah with willing submission, and feel themselves subdued."*--(Qur'an 9:29)

16

"O you who believe! Fight those of the disbelievers who are close to you, and let them find harshness in you, and know that Allah is with those who are the Al-Muttaqun."--(Qur'an 9:123)

Under Islamic rule, non-Muslims usually have three choices. Conversion to Islam, payment of a special tax (jizya), or death.[9]

Again, the Mohammedans were taught that Islam is the only path to God to motivate them to conquer their neighbours, to nation-build, and to justify the brutality that accompanies conquest. The Islamic Empires of the past, the fathers of the contemporary Islamic nations, were not created through persuasion or love, but more so by violence. Nor were they created in defense.[10] That's not to say Muslims can't live in harmony with people of other religions, they do and they have--typically, when radicalism isn't a nation's head and activating contradictory paragraphs. Even then, those who refuse to tolerate other faiths are few compared to the general public, and they do not pursue the passages in question. Nor are Muslims daily plotting to change the manner in which non-Muslims view life. Most of them overlook questionable canon and focus on the Godly ideas found within the *Qur'an.*

"Whoever saves the life of one human being, it shall be as if he had saved the whole of humankind"--(Qur'an 5:32)

"Those who believe and do good deeds--the Gracious God will create love in their hearts."--(Qur'an 19:97)

Through the use of propaganda designed to play with a person's loyalty to God, feelings such as fear, and the innate wants as outlined by Maslow in his Hierarchy of Needs, the political machine is what activates uncertain passages and misleads the believer to act on them. The political machine was also the force that inserted the questionable canon amongst Godly ideas in the first place. Secular motivations that even went as far as to oppress the female gender, when during Mohammad's time, women were regarded as equals.

The Hebrews and the Muslims are not the only people of God and the notions that suggest they are can only be political insertions designed to motivate the people to war and to conquer.

17

Godly messages were mixed with godless messages and presented as God sent, and unfortunately, the combination has existed for so long that it's evolved into a creature above rational debate. I'm sure that if a contest were to ensue, the reasonable person would conclude that it isn't the name of a religion that determines an individual's devotion but their state of awareness. God doesn't love religion. God loves the faithful.

In the end, every person has the right to harbour any belief they wish, but there is a difference between thoughts and actions.

Twisted Text: War

A large portion of the content within the different Holy Texts is God oriented. However, politically motivated insertions are plausible--injections easily twistable. These passages are few in relation to the entire content, but they're able to convince people to behave differently than the saintly would, and most horrific, to support war. Passages such as:

> *"Avenge the children of Israel of the Midianites: afterward shalt thou be gathered unto thy people."--(Numbers 31:2)*

> *"Think not that I am come to send peace on earth: I came not to send peace, but a sword."--(Matthew 10:34)*

> *"Give them according to their deeds, and according to the wickedness of their endeavours: give them after the work of their hands; render to them their desert."--(Psalms 28:4)*

> *"Or do you think that you will enter Paradise while Allah has not yet made evident those of you who fight in His cause and made evident those who are steadfast?"--(Qur'an 3:142)*

> *Who should determine whom to fight? Who should determine the causes prescribed by God? Who should determine what is evil and what is good? Those who determine can motivate the believers to any end they wish. For example, politicians can use the above passages to convince the flock to war against another nation. Politicians who do so will typically depict the nation they want to attack, or the governing body of that nation, as an evil. Then they'll link that evil to passages such as the above.*

Passages can also be used to convince a people to ignore the harm one group might be causing another, by associating such things as war to the End of Days, or to the Will of God.

> *"Then cometh the end, when he shall have delivered up the kingdom to God, even the Father; when he shall have put down all rule and all authority and power."--(Corinthians 15:24)*

"Say to those with fearful hearts, "Be strong, do not fear; your God will come, he will come with vengeance; with divine retribution he will come to save you."--(Isaiah 35:4)

"The four angels were released, who had been held ready for the hour, the day, the month, and the year, to kill a third of humankind."--(Rev 9:15)

"And the armies which are in heaven, clothed in fine linen, white and clean, were following Him on white horses. From His mouth comes a sharp sword, so that with it He may strike down the nations, and He will rule them with a rod of iron; and He treads the wine press of the fierce wrath of God, the Almighty. And on His robe and on His thigh He has a name written, 'KING OF KINGS, AND LORD OF LORDS.'"--(Rev 14-16)

"The angel swung his sickle on the earth, gathered its grapes and threw them into the great winepress of God's wrath."--(Rev 14:19)

"Fighting is prescribed for you, and ye dislike it. But it is possible that ye dislike a thing which is good for you, and that ye love a thing which is bad for you. But Allah knoweth, and ye know not."--(Qur'an 2:216)

The majority of the content within the Holy Texts is God oriented. Every person should study the Text(s) of their religion. A better understanding of The Great Architect will be the outcome. However, politically motivated insertions are evident. These passages are few in comparison to the entire content, but they have enough power that they can convince a person to behave anti-God.

The believer has little choice but to employ the art of critical thought when passages from a Holy Text are used to convince people to behave less than a child of God. Without critical thought, a person might accidentally subject the self to negative celestial consequence.

"You have heard that it was said, 'Love your neighbor and hate your enemy.' But I tell you, love your enemies and pray for those who persecute you, that you may be children of your Father in heaven. He causes his sun to rise on the evil and the good, and sends rain on the righteous and the unrighteous."--(Matthew 5:43-45)

Playing With Iron

Humanity is currently in the midst of the Iron Age. In this era, it is said that every institution built by man will eventually corrupt - regardless if the intention behind the creation is benevolent.

Some corrupt within a generation and others in several more. No government, religion, non-profit organization, or corporation is sheltered from the shadows, and no amount of earthly currency can buy protection from the Age of Iron.

God's People II

Regardless of how popular media presents it, the state of Israel sometimes behaves like those who attack them, and the fact of the matter is, after the Second World War, the United States, France, and Britain created the nation-state of Israel. In doing so, they immorally removed the Palestinians from parts of their homeland.

Even after the 1979 peace treaty between Israel and Palestine, in which the two sides agreed to a border and a cease-fire, Israel continued to take. That said; it could be that Israel continued to increase her size so to create a buffer zone between Israel and the terrorists who just won't stop attacking innocent Israelis. But, in doing so, and according to Sufyan Omeish and Abdallah Omeish in their video documentary, *Occupation 101: Voices of the Silenced Majority* (2006), Israel is illegally and unjustly invading and colonizing Palestinian land. In the process, Israel is forcefully removing Palestinians from their homes.

Imagine if that was happening where you live. What would you do if another people decided to use their military strength to remove you from your home and occupy your land?

Jimmy Carter, former President of the United States, in his book, *Palestine: Peace Not Apartheid* (2006), compares the Israeli Government to the apartheid government that once existed in South Africa.

Even some Israeli soldiers disagree with the occupation of Palestine--they think Israel is acting immorally (Journeyman Pictures, *Crisis of Conscience--Israel/Palestine*, 2002).

However, mainstream media doesn't present the Palestinian plight as righteous. Instead, they sometimes create a similar atmosphere to the "Two Minutes Hate" ritual in the novel, *1984*, by George Orwell. In that, they hide the innocent Palestinian faces killed in the madness and more so highlight the crazed Islamic terrorists.

It would seem that when they talk about peace in the Mid-East, what they're actually talking about is creating an environment where Israel can peacefully take away Palestinian land.

I can't help but feel that those Jewish people willing to invade, occupy, oppress, displace other human beings, or generate terror were inspired or desensitized by the scattered darkness found within the *Old Testament*, and by the idea that they are the people of God and no others are. They're trapped in an Iron Cage similar to what Max Weber once described, and to ideas that can only be political injections. Political insertions designed to motivate a group of people to nation build, to feel comfortable with the atrocities spurred in the process, and to desensitize them to violence. Passages such as:

> *"'Go up against the land of Merathaim, and against the inhabitants of Pekod. Kill, and devote them to destruction, declares the LORD, and do all that I have commanded you.'"*-- (Jeremiah 50:21)

> *"And while the children of Israel were in the wilderness, they found a man that gathered sticks upon the sabbath day. And they that found him gathering sticks brought him unto Moses and Aaron, and unto all the congregation. And they put him in ward, because it was not declared what should be done to him. And the Lord said unto Moses, The man shall be surely put to death: all the congregation shall stone him with stones without the camp. And all the congregation brought him without the camp, and stoned him with stones, and he died; as the Lord commanded Moses."*--(Numbers 15:32-36)

> *"When you march up to attack a city, make its people an offer of peace. If they accept and open their gates, all the people in it shall be subject to forced labour (slavery) and shall work for you. If they refuse to make peace and they engage you in battle, lay siege to that city. When the Lord your God delivers it into your hand, put to the sword all the men in it. As for the women, the children, the livestock and everything else in the city, you may take these as plunder for yourselves. And you may use the plunder the Lord your God gives you from your enemies. This is how you are to treat all the cities that are at a distance from you and do not belong to the nations nearby. However, in the cities of the nations the Lord your God is giving you as an inheritance, do not leave alive anything that breathes. Completely destroy them--the*

Hittites, Amorites, Canaanites, Perizzites, Hivites and Jebusites--
as the Lord your God has commanded you. Otherwise, they will
teach you to follow all the detestable things they do in worshiping
their gods, and you will sin against the Lord your God."--
(Deuteronomy 20:10-18)

Concepts that contradict violent behaviour can also be found within the Hebrew faith, and they are more in number than the questionable canon. But during times of conquest, they're abandoned by the political machine and more so remembered when there is no application required.

"When a stranger sojourns with you in your land, you shall not do
him wrong. You shall treat the stranger who sojourns with you as
the native among you, and you shall love him as yourself, for you
were strangers in the land of Egypt: I am the LORD your God."--
(Leviticus 19:33-34)

The events in the Middle-East are contemporary examples of the impact violent doctrine can have. No matter if the passages constitute only a tiny percentage of the overall message. The events are also an excellent example of the political influence over dogma.

The political manipulation has convinced the people of Israel that they have some sort of Divine right to the land there. Passages such as *Genesis 12:7* and *Genesis 15:18* are readily asserted. The supposed Godly passages appear to sanction the displacement and murder of the Palestinians.

Murder isn't the only anti-God element within the Jewish literature, as pointed to in a previous article, slavery is accepted by Jewish doctrine--complimented by an attitude of superiority. For example:

"Rab Judah said in the name of Samuel: The property of a
heathen (non-Jewish) is on the same footing as desert land;
whoever first occupies it acquires ownership."--(Babylonian
Talmud: Baba Bathra, Folio 54b)

"'Where a suit arises between an Israelite and a heathen (non-
Jewish), if you can justify the former according to the laws of
Israel, justify him and say: 'This is our law'; so also if you can

27

justify him by the laws of the heathens justify him and say [to the other party:] 'This is your law'; but if this cannot be done, we use subterfuges (deceptions) to circumvent him. "--(Babylonian Talmud: Baba Kamma, Folio 113a)

As in the case of Islam, not all the Hebrews value dark affirmations, but there are enough in positions of power to nullify the beliefs of the majority.

It is suggested that the political system, Zionism, is responsible for the carnage and not the Jewish people. There is a division of society in the state of Israel, between the rulers and the ruled. The latter, as in every nation and religion, are typically innocent victims of the selfish economic and political objectives of the former.

Eco-political intentions not only tricked the innocent people of Israel, Christendom too is convinced of Israel's heavenly right to occupy the Palestinian. Specifically, the Christians who believe the Jewish people are the chosen people. Christian nations such as America donate billions of dollars to Israel. Christians from around the world have also relocated to Israel to occupy lands taken from the Palestinians. There aren't enough Israelis to settle the stolen territory, and without a human presence, it's difficult to keep what's annexed--a fundamental understanding when attempting to build a nation. Like pawns, the people of Jesus are treated, but tragically, they believe differently. They believe they're fulfilling a holy mission.

Oddly, the idea of the Jewish people as God's people doesn't include the Christians. They're in the same boat as the rest of the people of the planet.

In the beginning, Britain, France, and America instigated the troubles between Palestine and Israel, and so much drama has taken place between the two that the idea of the freedom fighter and the terrorist are sometimes blurred. I think it's safe to say that all sides shelter both the terms. The Palestinians and the Israelis have both played the role of the terrorist. However, I think it's time that the Palestinians recognize the nation-state of Israel. Israel has a right to exist and they aren't going anywhere. But unfortunately, terror groups such as Hamas are misleading the Palestinian people, and Hamas does not desire peace. Surprisingly, Hamas will even kill fellow Palestinians if they behave outside Islamic notions. Hamas is completely barbaric--I've seen video footage of them shooting people for simply dancing. I also think that Israel should contribute to the peace process and cease her expansionist policy. Perhaps, if the two sides change their attitudes, peace in the Middle-East can be a reality.

The Pretender

Ignorant is thee who pretends to be. Separate they be from the better half in thee. Blind in mind they breathe and daily repeat. I speak of those who carry the name and symbols without the understanding.

An example of a pretender is a person who bares the symbols of a religion but terrorizes the innocent. Or a person who raps about The One Virtuous Lord in the same verse in which ungodly thoughts and behaviour are dancing.

We've all witnessed the pretenders and no religion is without the black marks. There isn't a religion in the world that the Age of Darkness didn't infiltrate.

The Age of Darkness, also known as the Age of Iron, highlighted in the second part of this chapter, has infiltrated religions and the pretender is a manifestation. With little knowledge of their faith's philosophy and narration, they carry the name as if it was a part of their disposition. In the process, they give a distorted definition.

Tragically, the distortion is wrongly influencing the newer generations, and the misdirection has wrongly given the outsiders looking in an inaccurate definition. Regrettably, the result has been a further alienation from the likes of the God sent, and the truth in their religions.

A faith is not a birthright. It is to be or not to be. All faiths are holy. It's a matter of being.

The Dark Side of the Church

For the days now gone, blame the generations who betrayed our innocence. Blame those who muddied religion that now fools the innocent.

It's more than evident that the truths proclaimed by some can't be trusted, and they can't be trusted because a selfish agenda motivated some to purposely corrupt them. The past British Empire is one of the biggest culprits. They're responsible for distorting historical and cultural knowledge, and injecting lies into the Empire's **collective intelligence.**[11] The British Empire did that to gain popular support for imperialism and to control what wasn't theirs to have. In the process, they corrupted the heritage of the world and polluted the minds of those who encountered them.

For example, with the rise of European colonialism and imperialism, the European decision-makers purposely injected untruthful information into their respective European cultures. That information depicted the coloured of the world as intellectually and morally inferior. They injected that type of information so to garnish their colonial and imperial motivations as acts of liberation and divine purpose, and to help their populace feel comfortable with the evil that accompanies occupation and exploitation.

Sometimes the colonialists ignored, sometimes they labelled, and sometimes they attempted to change what is. For example, when an interest in ancient Egypt first surfaced, the Europeans completely ignored the fact that there were once powerful Black Pharaohs in Egypt. Instead, they would depict them as light skinned. Europe makes the claim that the printing press and the compass are European innovations but the Chinese actually invented them. And the contemporary Western World credits the ancient Greek philosophers as the pioneers of thought but the fact remains that the Persian and the Indian philosophers came centuries before the likes of Aristotle. In actuality, the Greeks referenced them, including the greats such as Pythagoras, Socrates, and Zeno. The foundation of Western culture is not Greco-Roman but Indo-Persian.

Opportune for them, but tragic for the woman and man, the person is born unaware of the truth. Moreover, the human is born innocent and will trust almost all information presented as honest. As such, it's nearly impossible to know what isn't shown without digging through all the political rhetoric, the selfish insertions, and the out and out false information presented as honest.

To that end, some in the contemporary Western World do not see the British colonial era through the same prescription glasses, and the lenses they wear keep their vision slightly out of focus. What I'm suggesting is that the majority of the population were shown only the positive elements such as early industrialization, and they were given an inaccurate image that depicted the occupied as a morally, spiritually, economically, and intellectually inferior people. Needless to say, the British employed the **language of deliberate deception** and most people under their influence were victims of misinformation.

One of the most popular lies the British-history books like to propagate is that the British Empire was benevolent, and that's how they grew to be a world power. Unfortunately, the reality is much different. The British Empire reached the size it did because they destroyed people, local economies, customs, history, people, and righteous cultures in an attempt to fulfill their imperial agenda. There is no question that they employed deceit as if they were the shadows of the devil. Their demonic tactics are what allowed them to occupy other people.

For example, they would enter the territory that interested their imperial agenda and befriend the people of that nation, under the guise of friendship, honesty, truth, and mutual cooperation, they would learn the manner in which the leadership governed their people, the local culture, and the existing conflicts that divided the people. After which, they would network with those opposed to the governing body. When the opportunity presented itself, the British would use their knowledge to topple the governing body and then replace it with a body they could control. They would then enslave the locals and sully their economy, culture, political makeup, and spiritual customs. In addition, they murdered the unsuspecting on mass and pitted people against people if required to maintain their power.

During the time of colonialism, the language of deliberate deception was employed to garnish domestic support. Without support from the populace, it would have been impossible for the Crown to wage war and occupy other nations and people. If the domestic populace knew that the British Empire was slaying noble and just people who were of a noble and just society, the people of England would've risen up against such an ungodly endeavour. But they were misled to believe that the British were saving the people of the world from themselves and introducing superior moral, spiritual, economic, and intellectual principles rather than annihilating them. It's much easier to support conquest if the general population of the invader believe they're acting for the good of humanity. More so if they believe they're acting on behalf of God--an idea that was also conditioned and readily reinforced to motivate the people to overlook and even undertake ungodly acts.

Unfortunately, the British weren't the only culprits. Throughout the recorded centuries, many nations, religions, groups, and institutions the world over did the same. Another good example, on par with British colonialism, is the offspring of the Roman Empire, the Catholic Church.[12]

Based on historical accounts, the Roman Empire didn't fall but slowly transitioned into what is now the Catholic Church. After that, the Church used the language of deliberate deception, just as the British Empire did, to foster ideas that benefit the rulers and create an illusion. In the process, they readily behaved differently than Jesus did. For example, the Church:

1) Burned people on the stake... the Inquisitions. Countless innocent people were eliminated.

2) Deemed the woman as inferior and not equal, for example, "*St. Paul, in the first epistle to the Corinthians, condemns woman's participation in the exercises of worship and instruction in the Christian assemblies of Corinth.*"[13]

3) Persecuted the likes of Galileo for proclaiming that the earth didn't stand still and wasn't the center of the Universe.[14] They further convinced countless people that the third planet from the sun was flat and man could fall off the edge. Along with an inaccurate theory that suggests the formation of the planet happened 6000 years in the past.[15]

Under the watch of the Church, to keep the general public ignorant, knowledge was distorted. Knowledge is power and the Church, like the other religious institutions, isn't in the business of empowering their followers. Religions are instruments of the rulers to herd the ruled. Just like the institution of government sometimes is.

33

4) Openly attacked the Jewish people by proclaiming that they killed Jesus, and the Church used passages from *Scripture* to do it. Statements such as the one made by the Roman Procurator, Pontius Pilate, as he was washing his hands before a crowd of Jewish people who were calling for the death of the Saviour: *"I am innocent of this man's blood; see to it yourselves."*[16]

5) Murdered other Christians such as the noble Gnostics and Cathars.[17] The Church did that to consolidate their power as the only institution of Jesus. Groups such as the Cathars were openly denying the divine authority of the Pope, and teaching a doctrine faithful to the *Scriptures*--propositions that threatened the power of the Church.

Before, during, and after the killing of all competing groups, the Church branded them as an evil. Seventeen-hundred years later and still those groups are remembered as the devil's minions.

The Church typically labels most other religious groups able to threaten their power as anti-God, and the Church is known to discredit knowledge that could empower a person. An empowered individual has little need for an intermediary establishment, and an empowered person has the potential to challenge the authority of the rulers. It would be reasonable to examine the knowledge they discredit and determine the value of it for the self.

The Catholic Church isn't the only entity that attacked knowledge able to liberate a person, and all ruling parties from all over the world did the same. The storehouses of wisdom such as the Library of Alexandria, the magnificent Library of Nalanda, the Mayan libraries of the Yucatan, the Library of Al-Hakam II, the Xianyang Palace Library, the American Library of Congress in 1814, and the Sikh Reference Library in 1984 were destroyed for that reason.

However, when it isn't possible to eradicate knowledge, the powerful will infiltrate the institution built to communicate that knowledge, and from within they will manipulate the information delivered to the general public--concealing the knowledge able to enhance a person's awareness of the self and the world. Furthermore, they will popularize information designed to misdirect the truth seeker.

6) Denied all knowledge of Jesus and Christianity that they themselves didn't package and cater, for example:

a. It's more than plausible that Jesus Christ traveled to India during his missing years[18] but the Church can't accept the possibility that Jesus mingled with Indian holy men.

b. The evidence suggests that Jesus wasn't born on December 25th but the Catholic Church ignores the data. The Church ignores the suggestion because if the Church acknowledges the possibility, the Church will be revealed as fallible and not so divine.

The evidence hints that the date December 25th was given by the Roman Empire to appease the Pagan population and their sun god, at a time when Christianity was still young and looking for converts.[19] That said, the date of his birth doesn't truly matter. It's his life that should be remembered. Focus your consciousness on the Christ Consciousness every day and not just on a particular day or month.

c. Destroyed dozens of competing Christian *Gospels* after the creation of the *New Testament.*

7) Assisted Hitler's henchmen during World War II, and factions of the Church helped several Nazis escape post-war judgement.[20]

8) Forcefully converted the First Nations people to Catholicism, so to eliminate their cultures. The Catholic Residential Schools, built to achieve that end, are remembered by the First Nations people as places of torture, murder, and abuse.

9) Hunted any advanced philosophy such as the one developed by Hermes Trismegistus. All schools that taught his knowledge were reduced to ashes.

10) With the help of the Spanish Empire, tortured and sacrificed the Aztec and Inca people. They exterminated tens-of-millions.

The Church's actions have repeatedly proven that it is first a political mechanism before a true religious institution. However, they present themselves as an instrument of God before an instrument of self-interest. Even the *New Testament* is secondary to their political will. They've demonstrated that by institutionalizing doctrine that isn't *New Testament.* It would appear

35

that they're more so concerned with control and not the enlightenment of their followers. For example, the Church:

1) Created dogma like Purgatory,[21] Indulgences, and Auricular Confessions,[22] and purposely tricked the human spirit.

a. The idea of Purgatory was created as an instrument of fear and control, and it was actually first introduced by two Greek inventors in the second century, Clement of Alexandria and Origen.[23] Afterward, it evolved into its present form.

b. To compliment the idea of Purgatory and to reinforce their power, the leaders of the Church also created another tool of control called Indulgences. Indulgences were pieces of paper with Latin writing on them that reduced the amount of time a person would spend in Purgatory. Only an individual ordained by the Catholic Church was able to issue them. They normally issued them for a price.

c. And the Confessional was designed as an apparatus for the guilty to turn him or herself in. Moreover, it was a mechanism to reinforce the Church's position as God's sole representative, and as a device for the priests to exercise authority and control over the common people. In his book, *The History of the Confessional*, John Henry Hopkins states, *"it is in the Confessional that the priesthood wields their vast and secret power over the people. It is by the Confessional that they rivet the chains of superstition upon the conscience and the soul."*[24]

2) Portrayed an image of Jesus as a common man with a common weakness by convincing their members that Jesus drank wine. The holy ones like Jesus didn't need or desire a material substance to alter their state of mind.

Wine was given to the flock by the Church to get them "high" and to keep them easily susceptible, not for their benefit, and let's not forget that intoxicated people are looser with their wallets. I guess someone forgot *Ephesians 5:18*, and *Luke 1:15*: *"Do not get drunk on wine, which leads to debauchery. Instead, be filled with the Spirit."*--(Ephesians 5:18) *"For he will be great in the sight of the Lord. He is never to take wine or other fermented drink, and he will be filled with the Holy Spirit even before he is born."*--(Luke 1:15)

3) Fixated the Catholic consciousness more on the vessel than the spark that was within, and the Catholic Church seems to give more importance to Jesus' mother, Mary, than Jesus.

By pushing ideas that focus the consciousness away from the Christ Consciousness, an individual doesn't receive the same blessings as they would by focusing on the Christ Consciousness. It would appear that the Catholic institution accidentally or purposely disempowered the potential of the Catholic people. Don't get me wrong, Mary was amazing and she carried Jesus. It's important to remember the vessel but not more so than "The Light" that was within.

It's also fair to mention that the Virgin Mary wasn't the only virgin mother. Krishna and others are acclaimed as sons of virgins.[25]

4) Created a vast administrative infrastructure (cardinals, archbishops, archdeacons, priests, monks, nuns, etc.) which is unscriptural. *"The Church, in the sense of the clergy, is not to be found in the whole Bible."*[26] It can be said that they created their grand institution to present themselves as the only gateway to The Eternal and to legitimize their existence. In keeping with this idea, for centuries they presented themselves as the only entity authorized to interpret the *Scriptures*. That wrongly led to a monopoly over the holy literature, which in turn wrongly strengthened their position as the only entity capable of interpreting the *Bible* and communing with The Formless Lord.

It would seem that the simplicity of Jesus' Church was lost to Roman secularism, ambition, and politics. Jesus never envisioned such a grand infrastructure and hierarchy, as presented by the Holy-Roman Catholic Church, to mediate the affairs of God. However, a massive infrastructure does help control the ruled and consolidate the power of the rulers.

5) And convinced the Catholics that God appoints the Pope and the Pope is The Great Architect's earthly representative. However, the belief isn't scriptural and the *Bible* actually speaks against an earthly head. *"But do not be called Rabbi; for One is your Teacher, and you are all brothers. Do not call anyone on earth your father; for One is your Father, He who is in heaven."*-- (Matthew 23:8-9).

There was a time when the appointment of a Pope was actually approved by the Roman Emperor.[27] The Pope is as ordained as King James or **Caligula** were, and they all proclaimed a divine right so to maintain and enhance their power, wealth, and control. The same applies to the Papacy. The people were taught to think of the Pope as appointed by God to limit any resistance to the Catholic Church's authority.

The Catholic Church and the Pope expect complete submission and obedience from their followers, even when they've behaved in corrupt, scandalous, immoral, and fallible ways.[28] Under the leadership of the Popes, the world within their grasp went through centuries of darkness. From the 4th to the 15th century, the Church dominated the nations that were under her influence, and in that time period, civilizations regressed. It was a period of feeble-mindedness known as the age of darkness. The damage done during that time is still with the Christian world. Kingdoms like the Ottoman Empire didn't do much better, and the advancements they did demonstrate were not native developments but mostly inventions they took from the people they invaded. Of which, substantial knowledge was dismissed because it wasn't permitted by their governing ideology.

The Catholic Church is the largest and wealthiest religion in the world, but unfortunately, they've behaved as most other empires have. They manipulated the beliefs of those they could so to expand and maintain their power, wealth, and control. The supposed truths communicated by the Church might not be so truthful.

I'm not certain when the Church first decided to stage-manage their followers, but if I had to make a guess, I would suggest that it was soon after the Roman Empire took an interest in the establishment.

Sometime in the 300s, the Roman Empire took control of what is now the Catholic Church. After which is when the Church created the *New Testament* and began murdering other Christians and destroying other Christian *Gospels*. They were attempting to consolidate their influence. Like drug-dealers who murder the competition to expand their market share.

It should be remembered that the Roman Empire, before the conversion to Christendom, worked to eliminate every Christian from the Roman dominion because the Christians were not so easily ruled by Roman values. The Roman

38

values questioned by the House of Jesus were those that condoned the exploitation, slavery, murder, and thievery of others. Fortunately, the Roman Empire was unable to eliminate the Christians. Mystically, Christendom continued to multiple. With the killing of one Christian, two would rise to take his or her place. Persecuting the Christians only provoked the growth of the faith.

Unfortunately, the Romans employed another tactic when the first failed. They strategically infiltrated Christendom. Instead of attempting to wipe the Christians off the face of the earth, the Empire embraced them, became them, and took control of them from within. Burdening the Christians not only with a secular leadership, but also with the luggage the Empire brought with it. For example, the fight between the Catholics and the Muslims is a carry-over of the conflict between Rome and the Persian Empire. Islam conquered the territories of the Persian's, and the Catholic Church inherited the property of Rome. The elites of those lands still held a grudge and continued the struggle but under a different banner.

It's difficult to deny that the Church was infiltrated by political ambitions and that happening led to corrupt and fallible behaviour. That happening is also responsible for the decline in the belief of God. Religion has deceived people one too many times and the mass exodus was the reaction to the lies. Regrettably, those who stepped outside the Church had few options to turn to. The Church dominates the religious market.

Nonetheless, don't be mistaken, their shady behaviour isn't an indication that there is no God, nor is it an indication that the Church facilitates zero truth. As in the case of Islam, the truths of the metaphysical are far more prevalent than the fabrications and the political injections. It's a matter of distinguishing between truths and falsehoods, and understanding religion as a political mechanism before a servant of God.

By addressing the politics played by, for example, the Church, a person only steps that much closer to The Formless. Concurrently, the arguments put forth to deny God are effectively neutralized. God is self-evident and there is no viable argument that denies God--individuals such as Richard Dawkins try but their arguments fall short. Likewise, the corruption of religion is self-evident, and the corruption of religion is what individuals such as Dawkins depend on to deny The Great Architect. Popular culture too highlights the corruption of religion to imply that there is no God. But their logic is flawed. There is a distinction between God and religion.

Acknowledging the corruption also gives rise to the opportunity to correct the divergence and to return to the humble and universal nature that is the Church of Jesus--before the corporate infrastructure, the countless administrators, the political injections, the divisions, and the selfish ambitions.

The Church acts more like a political and economic institution than an instrument of Jesus, but that isn't to say that the followers of the Church are politically motivated or selfish. The followers of the Church are good people with good intentions. The true Catholic, like the true Muslim and the true Hebrew, efforts to live a God oriented life, and as with all of them, there is a distinction between the institution and the people. With that in mind, this manuscript challenges religious institutions and not their members. The follower did what every person should do and he or she went looking for God. It isn't the members I question but the institutions. I question them when they take advantage of a person's innocence and willingness to follow.

After speaking with a few Catholic friends about such things as the crusades, the Spanish Inquisition, and the atrocities committed towards the First Nations, they were passively aware of the corruption within the Church and felt very much ashamed and helpless. They were able to draw the distinction between the politically motivated and the celestially inspired, but felt as if they were powerless to exorcize the Church of its political component. To the detriment of the God seeker, a mist surrounds the nature of the Church.

The corruptions of the Church are obvious, and the Church is an excellent example of a religion that unjustly presents itself as incorruptible, but can be proven opposite. Other religious institutions also have their share of dirt. They too house similar examples. They too were infiltrated. For that reason, it would be reasonable for a person to question the doctrine and the history written by people, groups, nations, or institutions that repeatedly acted corruptly. It would also be reasonable for a person to attempt to discover truths through other sources and then get back to their faith. It would be sensible to exercise the only real option available and rationally rebuild. A temporary separation of God and religion is required.

However, there is no need to question all information presented by religions. Examine the stuff that stimulates feelings of discomfort, divides people from people, pits one against another, condones violence, glorifies plunder, disregards the humanity of a people or person, challenges reasonable knowledge, restricts the unlimited power of The Formless, provokes a sense of fear to gain obedience, exemplifies an economic agenda, denies the truth in other religions, or promotes institutional mediation to connect with the heavens.

Although the corruptions and the deceptions of the "post-Roman" Catholic Church are used to make a general point about religious institutions, again, the Catholic Church does teach the truths pertaining to the celestial--just like every other religion does. They've also produced amazing holy saints such as St Francis, St George, and St Simeon Stylites. Not only that, because of the astronomical amount of wealth the Church possesses, the Church has the potential to be the greatest of virtuous institutions the world has ever seen. But first, they would have to apologize for the many devilish deeds carried out in the name of religion--a confession that seems unlikely. To admit that mistakes were made is to admit the Church is fallible and not divine. For what is divine is infallible and forever truthful. If a religious institution is repeatedly proven corrupt, the people will naturally question the remainder of the doctrine they've pushed. That would obviously threaten the power of the Church and their ability to motivate a people to behave in a specific way.

If I were to make a recommendation, it would not include walking away from the Catholic Church. That would only create more denominations. The reason they came about in the first place. Further disunity isn't the solution, and an examination of the Church is required. But seventeen-hundred years of political games echo the halls of the Vatican, where to begin to clean the contamination?

St Francis could talk to animals and calm beasts. He was also habitually subject to the stigmata, and he did what he could to keep the Church from straying.

St George is one of the most recognized Christian military saints and one of the bravest martyrs of Christendom. As a soldier in Diocletian's army, in early 300 AD, George was instructed to renounce his faith and adopt the Pagan

41

belief system. On his refusal, he was executed, but not before giving all his wealth to the poor.

St Simeon Stylites spent 40 days in a hut without any food or water. This is a common story found in other religions, and only those touched by The Eternal are able to perform such a feat. The human condition houses an organ that produces the nutrients a person needs to live, and the saints who are able to live without food and water for a prolonged period of time were granted access to that specific organ by The Eternal.

The British actively distorted cultural and historical truths to further their imperialistic agenda. It can be said that most of the empires that came and went also practiced the art of conditioning falsehoods.[29] Maybe, that's why the descendants of the Roman Empire, the Church, did it too. In the end, they all had the same goal in mind, to place themselves as supreme in the conquered cultures literature and thought. That was done to legitimize and strengthen their hold over the general public and the generations to come. Generations bred ignorant to the truth can't challenge and only God knows the true extent of the deception. Likewise, most people are born into religion and haven't truly endeavoured to discover what The Formless is, and innocently, some believe in the political spin that's presented as God sent.

"Jesus said, 'The Pharisees and the scribes have taken the keys of Knowledge and hidden them. They themselves have not entered, nor have they allowed to enter those who wish to. You, however, be as wise as serpents and as innocent as doves.'"--(Gospel of Thomas)

Religion was infiltrated and employed by the elite ruling class to take a flock's wealth, to motivate a people to war and to plunder; to alienate the general public from ideas and knowledge that might bring them to a better understanding of God, to propagate fear, to control the herd, and to reinforce their status as the upper class. The footprints left by the infiltration are more than evident. Religions were corrupted. However, that isn't to suggest that God is. Friend, there is a distinction.

Enemies

A common enemy has united nations. A common enemy can unite the world. Do not look to another to see an enemy, look to the ways of the world.

Poverty--Hunger--Illiteracy. Consumption--Waste--Pollution. Jealousy--Hate--Divisions. Greed--War--Oppression.

"A new command I give you: Love one another. As I have loved you, so you must love one another. By this everyone will know that you are my disciples, if you love one another."--(John 13:34-35)

Twisted Text: End of Days

Some groups twisted the passages in their Text and convinced the faithful to Jihad. They forgot that the murder of the innocent accompanies negative celestial consequence, and not a flock of virgins.

Some groups twisted the passages in their Text and now people wail against a wall to please The Formless. They idolize as if they forgot the magnificent Moses.

Some groups twisted the passages in their Text and subjugated the female. They oppressed the gender who gave the world the likes of Nanak, Buddha, Mohammad, and Jesus.

Some groups twisted the passages in their Text and turned a faithful into a prostitute (Mary Magdalene).[30] They attempt to rob the human potential.

Some groups twisted the passages in their Text and made hatred holy. They justified racism and the enslavement of the African[31] by suggesting, for example, the mark of Cain, discussed in *Genesis 4*, is the reason the Africans are dark-skinned. The Africans were depicted as the descendents of the evil Cain, and because they were, their enslavement was sanctioned. I guess they were oblivious to the fact that the face of Jesus was also painted.

Some groups twisted the passages in their Text and now act as if global warming is an indication of the end and a Godly phenomenon. They ignore the fact that the effect is manmade and humanity has the power to reverse the damage they've done. They, instead of protecting our First Mother, protect those who pollute and plunder. They do that by pretending the damage large corporations do to the planet, in their search for more profit, is an act of The Eternal.

And some groups twisted the passages in their Text and persuaded their congregation that God is hell bent. They comically wait in excited anticipation for the days to end. More than 2 millennia have passed and some are still under the impression that the end of days will come tomorrow or the next.[32] Similar in comparison to when most thought that the earth was flat--people are misled but assume they're on the right track. Ironically, almost every generation has a group who thinks their generation will be the last, and they all point to the negative world events of their time as the indicators of the end.[33]

But even more shocking, there are actually some who work to bring forth the **Apocalypse**, or what the Hebrews call "the Eschaton", like Captain Ahab chased Moby Dick. Although the majority of the people who believe in Judgment Day aren't obsessed with bringing it forth, there are those, categorized as "activists", who actively seek to bring about the end.[34] Intoxicated by the illusion of a heavenly will,[35] they plot, scheme, and fuel wars to create the circumstances and material things necessary to usher in the Day of Judgment. Circumstances like the complete occupation of the "Promised Land" by the Jewish people,[36] and material things like the Temple of Solomon.[37]

Coincidentally, half of the "Promised Land" is home to Muslims (the Palestinians), and the place where the fundamentalists have indicated that the Temple of Solomon must be is the exact place where the Temple Mount is. The Temple Mount is one of the holiest sites in Islam. Can you see the problem? But bloodshed is anticipated by the seekers of Apocalypse.[38] They fully accept the fact that millions must die for them to live in the Kingdom of Heaven. They fully believe that mass murder is a precursor to their happiness--readily disguising it as a battle against evil and the "Will" of God.[39]

The activists aren't satisfied with God's timeline, and instead, they believe that they can provoke God into acting.

I'm sure there will be an end to humanity. Everything that has a beginning has an end (excluding The Eternal). But that end time is not for humanity to determine. When God is ready to end humanity, I'm sure God will, and since The Formless is infinitely stronger than every person combined together is, I don't think God would need mere mortals to carry out the plan. As for the Kingdom of Heaven, take a read at what Jesus had to say about the topic.

> *"His disciples said to Him, 'When will the repose of the dead come about, and when will the new world come?' He said to them, 'What you look forward to has already come, but you do not recognize it.'"*--(Gospel of Thomas)

Luke further explains:

"And when he was demanded of the Pharisees, when the kingdom of God should come, he answered them and said, The kingdom of God cometh not with observation: Neither shall they say, Lo here! or, lo there! for, behold, the kingdom of God is within you."-- (Luke 17:20-21)

I ask--is doctrine so easily twisted actually the ideas and words of God as each believes, or were they political insertions placed amongst Godly doctrine and taught as truth to deceive?

"Cruel men believe in a cruel God and use their belief to excuse their cruelty. Only kindly men believe in a kindly God, and they would be kindly in any case."--Bertrand Russell (1953)

Jesus never wrote the *Gospels*. Nor did Mohammad write the *Qur'an*. For that reason, the arrangement of words, sentences, and paragraphs in the *Bible* and the *Qur'an* are open to interpretation.

If Jesus had written the *Gospels*, if Mohammad had written the *Qur'an*, and if they were perfectly transmitted generation to generation, there would be no confusion, no denomination, and no twisting of the text.

<u>In Search of God</u>

A person will search for God when times are tough. But when times are tough, a person is typically weak in mind and susceptible. In such a state, a person will move toward what's easily available, and a person will most likely believe almost anyone who gives even a glimpse of hope. Tell me, what else explains the religious suicide cults like Heaven's Gate, Jonestown, and the **Order of the Solar Temple**? What else explains the door-to-door bible thumper?

On the latter, they believe that they're doing the work of God by attempting to increase their denomination's membership. They fail to recognize that they're actually working on behalf of the denomination's administration to increase donations and fatten their pockets.

The denominations that do encourage door-to-door thumping typically send the innocent. Based on my observations, it would appear that they send out the members who look most innocent and trustworthy like elderly women and young children. They exploit innocence like the media exploits promiscuity.

My viewpoint of the door-to-door bible thumper is based on my observations of "the doom" group known as the Jehovah's Witnesses, and they're one of many who like to push the propaganda that the world is about to end.

This *Scripture*-inspired denomination of Christianity has been in the business of prophesising for over a century, and "doomsday" is the reason they came to be. Originally, they believed that Jesus Christ, in 1874, came again in his second invisible presence[40] and the world would end in 1914 with Jesus Christ as the Supreme Authority of all world governments.[41] When 1914 came and went, they predicted a new date, 1915,[42] and when 1915 came and went, another date was predicted, 1918. Again, when that date was proven inaccurate, a new date was set for the beginning of the end of days, 1925.[43] Not surprisingly, that date too came and went. But surprisingly, some Jehovah's Witnesses still continue to fall for the propaganda that Armageddon is just around the bend.[44] Them are easily exploited and this religious institution readily twists the Text to suit an end-of-days prediction.

I have to say, the Jehovah's Witnesses do attempt to live a life governed by the better half of the mind, and it's not the follower I'm wondering about, for they are God seekers, it's the institution that is Jehovah's Witnesses, and their willingness to exploit and scare the person that troubles me.

A person will search for God when times are tough. However, when times are tough, a person is usually weak in mind and susceptible, and some religions behave like predators.

The Doctrine Within

Sometimes it's arduous determining what's what, especially when there's a preacher, pastor, mullah, brahmin, or minister countering all reasonable questions with the phrase, "just have faith". However, a person like me has faith and a person like me loves The Formless. But a person like me can't ignore the crooked politics played and the manner in which elements of some doctrine challenge the soul. Inspire they do feelings of confusion and discomfort.

I guess, at times, I'm a little too headstrong to allow the rhetoric to shut down my mind and the Inner Light. I can't accept everything presented as God sent. And from the looks of it, it appears that I'm not the only one. From the looks of it, I'm not the only one who can't ignore the spiritual, biological, and cognitive reactions.

I've spoken with many who also experience the same. They too feel as if something inside of them activates when they attempt to comprehend elements of some doctrine, like a house alarm after a parameter breach. I've spoken with many who've also experienced the same. They too felt as if something inside of them was intrinsically privy to the true nature of The Supreme Light, and when that nature is under question or information opposite to that intrinsic information is absorbed by the mind, that something activates feelings of confusion and discomfort--to alert the person of potential danger.

The inner alarm is what makes it arduous, and the inner alarm is what sways a person like me to question the preachers, pastors, mullahs, brahmins, and ministers. Their logic sometimes sounds like spin, the type propagated by G.W. Bush when he was trying to convince the Americans that Iraq possessed weapons of mass destruction. And when I hear them counter my reasonable questions with phrases like, "just have faith", it feels as if they're working to convince me that one plus one equals four.

Every individual is born with this intrinsic alarm, and it's designed to assist the person in his or her search for God knowledge. However, it can be hidden, just as **Mencius** believed that the good in a person could be disguised. In this case, inaccurately constructed God knowledge can bury the intrinsic alarm. If that happens, an individual's value system is ripe to justify happenings such as the crusades, the conversion of all non-Muslims, the repression of the Indigenous, the murder of the Cathars, bloodshed in Jerusalem, and a man-induced Armageddon.

Advantageously, just as the good in a person can be again, as Mencius suggested, with the appropriate nourishment, how can the buds and sprouts of the intrinsic not again appear?

Sometimes it's arduous determining what's what, especially when there's a preacher, pastor, mullah, brahmin, or minister countering all reasonable questions with the phrase, "just have faith". However, a person like me has faith and a person like me loves The Formless. But a person like me can't ignore the crooked politics played and the manner in which elements of some doctrine challenge the soul. Inspire they do feelings of confusion and discomfort.

<u>Elysian</u>

There exists God inspired dogma and there exists doctrine that doesn't have the same feel. The Godly inspires an aura of peace and harmony within, and the opposite inspires an aura of discomfort. I do not question the doctrine that brings peace and harmony to the "I" in me, but I can't help but question dogma that doesn't.

I can't help but question because only in truth is there salvation for the soul. For if I misinterpret the Universal principles that govern life and death, the "truest me" might not progress and advance like the "truest me" was meant to.

Like a caterpillar without the cocoon. Like a seed that wasn't sowed. Like a fool that threw away a gift from The Eternal.

Godly ideas are in every religion, and it is to them a person should give their allegiance. All ideas outside of them, no matter the paragraph before and after, are political creations.

Chapter 1
Part II: Canon Reloaded

Why this illusiveness, what's the intention, and how to become and finally break the silence? Tell me, is there a dance I can do to catch your attention? Words I can recite to gain your affection? Clothes I can wear for you to love me? A particular building where hidden they keep Thee? Or a specific name through which to feel your energy? Tell me, which chapter and in which book? Please, where to look?

God's Words

The most outspoken religious institutions--Christianity, Judaism, and Islam--repeatedly claim that their Holy Texts contain the only Words and Ideas of God. Absolute and incorrupt. Each also claims that their doctrine is the only path to The Formless. To my knowledge, the other popular religions of the world such as Sikhism, Buddhism, Hinduism, Jainism, and almost all ancient religions do not claim a monopoly over God knowledge.

However, in the case of the *New Testament*, Jesus never wrote what he thought or preached and words were attributed to him decades after he ascended into "The White Light". Men other then he wrote the *Gospels* and each writer plausibly mixed in his own personality. Clear evidence of that are the disagreements and the contradictions between the different versions of the *Bible*, such as those between the Latin Vulgate and the King James Version. And clear confirmation of that are the inconsistencies between the authors of the *Gospels*.

> "Mark says that Jesus was crucified the day after the Passover meal was eaten (Mark 14:12; 15:25) and John says he died the day before it was eaten (John 19:14)... Luke indicates in his account of Jesus's birth that Joseph and Mary returned to Nazareth just over a month after they had come to Bethlehem and performed the rites of purification (Luke 2:39), whereas Mathew indicates they instead fled to Egypt (Matt. 2:19-22)."[45]

Even though names are given, there is no way to confirm who actually wrote the *New Testament*,[46] and author Jack Nelson-Pallmeyer, in his book, *Is Religion Killing Us?: Violence in the Bible and the Quran* (2005), makes an interesting observation about one of the supposed, Mathew.

> "Matthew is often an unreliable witness of Jesus. In his parables Jesus repeatedly exposes key actors in the oppressive system, only to have Matthew present those exposed as 'God figures' that Matthew blesses with the authority of Jesus' voice. These 'God figures' consistently send people to the torturers or to other terrible punishments."

In all fairness, it's very possible that the authors of the *Gospels* were guided by a Divine Will, and thus making their words the Words of God. But the originals are lost and over the centuries words where changed, translated, dropped, or added. What we have today is not what originally was and maybe that's why there are contradictions. Author John Vaughan asserts:

> "...the original writers were preserved from all error by the direct assistance of the Holy Ghost, this Divine assistance does not extend to the individual monks or friars, or other scribes, however holy, who sat down, pen in hand, to reproduce the original text."[47]

Furthermore, the *Gospels* were initially communicated orally[48] and when the practice of recording them in writing came to be, unintentional and intentional mistakes were made.

> "...scribes occasionally altered the words of their sacred texts to make them more patently orthodox."[49]

> "At times scribes would make intentional changes as they copied. For example, they would correct what they believed to be a spelling error in their source text. And even the best of scribes also sometimes made unintended errors."[50]

> "There were thousands and thousands of copyists busily employed in the monasteries and scriptoriums through the world. Through want of observation or through carelessness or weariness, or on account of difficult or partially effaced writing, how easy it was to mistake a letter, or to omit a word or a particle; yet such an omission is capable of altogether changing the sense of an entire passage. The accidental dropping of even a single letter may sometimes make a striking difference."[51]

> "Attestations of variants within the lectionary tradition are so manifold that there is little plausibility in the theory that at the beginning of the lectionary tradition there was one specific text set up for liturgical reading that was then copied as a unity and in the course of its history increasingly brought into agreement with the mainstream. It appears to be more likely that different text

forms fed into the lectionary tradition and were carefully copied and 'commonly and officially used.'"[52]

In relation, the contemporary English *Gospels* are all translations of translations of translations,[53] and the original *Gospels* didn't survive. What we have are translations of copies of the originals and not translations of the originals (autographs).[54] Bart Ehrman, an expert on the topic, writes:

> *"So rather than actually having the inspired words of the autographs (i.e., the originals) of the Bible, what we have are the error-ridden copies of the autographs."*[55]

> *"We have only error-ridden copies, and the vast majority of these are centuries removed from the originals and different from them, evidently, in thousands of ways."*[56]

> *"What good does it do to say that the words are inspired by God if most people have absolutely no access to these words, but only to more or less clumsy renderings of these words into a language, such as English, that has nothing to do with the original words?"*[57]

Three centuries after the death of Jesus, under the guidance of Emperor Constantine (a politician), the Christian doctrine was solidified. But during the process, not all of the *Gospels* were included and knowledge was purposely hidden.[58] And debated doctrine such as--was Jesus God, the Son of God, or a mortal man--were arbitrarily put to rest by one person who was allegedly considered a heretic by the Christians,[59] and who's been repeatedly proven inaccurate by contemporary historians, Eusebius, the Emperor's religious advisor.[60] It's a fact that before Constantine consolidated the Christian doctrine, *"thousands of documents existed chronicling His life (Jesus' life) as a mortal man."*[61]

So, why would an emperor want to ally himself with God, or the Son of God, and not a mortal man? The answer is simple. God and the Son are more powerful than any man is. It's always more advantageous to ally with the more powerful.

Not only was the above doctrine challenged, many Christians also questioned dogma like that presented in *Apocalypse* (*Book of Revelation*). They considered it sacrilegious.[62]

Now, why would Constantine want such literature as part of the Christian doctrine? Divine punishment is required to keep the people obedient and dependent on the institution providing the means to salvation from that divine punishment. *Apocalypse* provides very descriptive images of that divine punishment. Those images create vivid pictures within the mind. That experience reinforces the overall idea of a divine punishment. Also, as every good emperor knows, the people must be willing to act violently to maintain and expand an empire. The violence within *Apocalypse* desensitizes a people to violence, and contributes to that end.

It should be noted that before Constantine, the Christians were persecuted by the Roman Empire and their sacred books were destroyed. Not all of the recorded truths of Jesus and Christianity were available when Constantine decided to consolidate the Christian faith.[63]

During the melding process, there were Christians who didn't agree with Constantine's version of Christianity. However, they didn't object because they feared that the Emperor would punish them. Two actually did disagree and they were exiled.[64]

After Constantine's interference, what is now the Catholic Church remained and all other types of Christianity were persecuted,[65] and all competing *Gospels* were destroyed.[66] Any person or group opposed to the doctrine and *Bible* presented by the Church where depicted as an evil and then eliminated.

Before Constantine, the different Christian perspectives debated but they rarely resorted to violence. Even though some people propagated horrid opinions.[67]

> *"Blessed are the peacemakers, for they shall be called sons of God."*--(Matthew 5:9)

But after Constantine, violence was used to consolidate the *New Testament* and the power of those who held it. Something I think Jesus would probably disagree with. He believed in peace and not violence as the instrument best equipped to reveal God's Kingdom.

The unification of Christianity also included the conversion of the Catholic clergy into employees of Rome.[68] Afterward, they took the titles of the Roman Government, and they changed in demeanour to reflect their Roman status.[69] As you can guess, after the Romans gave importance to the Church, the Church began attracting power and wealth. Subsequently, *"power-hungry, greedy politicians began to take over positions of leadership".*[70]

Author David L. Dungan astutely recaps Constantine's interference in his book, *Constantine's Bible: politics and the making of the New Testament* (Fortress Press: Philadelphia, 2006).

> *"...the newly Christian emperor's efforts to influence virtually every aspect of his newfound ally, Catholic Christianity – from building new churches to paying clergy out of the state treasury, to intervening in church disputes, to convening councils of bishops and issuing edicts and making their decisions the law of the realm, to helping to determine the date for celebrating Easter to mandating Sunday as the universal day of worship, to outlawing heresy, to de facto implementations of Eusebius's 'acknowledged books' as the standard Bible of the Catholic Church."*--Page 94-95.

Although the Church suggests that the *Bible* is constituted by the only Words of God, the *Bible* doesn't make that assertion.[71] The Church, like the other popular religions, teaches that idea so to squash a person's logic, to limit any resistance, to pit one against another, to hide truth, to empire-build, and to disguise their political agenda and spin.

Regardless, the *Gospels* are still valuable and they're precious in the sense that they communicate important lessons and messages. They teach a person to live a moral, virtuous, and God orientated lifestyle. I was born and raised amongst the Christians and the true Christian is a person of excellent character. But to say that the *New Testament* is the only book with uncorrupted truth and the only that contains the Words of The Formless is inaccurate.

Judaism

Judaism also believes that their Texts are the only path to the truth and the only Words of God. However, Judaism suffers from the same problem Christianity does.

> *"The original text of Moses, and the ancient prophets, was destroyed with the temple and city of Jerusalem, by the Assyrians under Nebuchadnezzar; and the authentic copies which replaced them, perished in the persecution of Antiochus."[72]*

> *"There is no original manuscript of the Bible extant anywhere throughout the world. All that we now possess are copies. Though the Old Testament writings were written three thousand years and more ago, we have no existing manuscript of the Hebrew Old Testament earlier than the ninth or tenth century after Christ."[73]*

> *"Believers like to think of 'sacred' texts as God's words, or at least as words inspired by God, but elite priestly writers were often guided by self-interest. They reinforced their own power by writing their privileges into the 'sacred' text." As Richard Horsley argues, the "'Priestly writers' of early postexilic times (when the Hebrew Scriptures were compiled and edited) reconstructed and virtually established a religious tradition as a way of legitimating the 'restored' Jewish social-political order."[74]*

Moreover, pieces of the *Old Testament* justify violence and immorality in the pursuit of a nation. I guess it's easier to convince people to kill other people and to take what they have, if God said they should kill and take.

> *"God, according to the Hebrew Scriptures, is a determined and powerful land thief who steals from others in order to give to the chosen people 'To your (Abram's) descendants I give this land, from the river of Egypt to the great river, the river Euphrates, the land of the Kenites, the Kenizzites, the Kadmonites, the Hittites, the Perizzites, the Rephiam, the Amorites, the Canaanites, the Girgashites, and Jebusites' (Gen 15:18-21). God-ordained land thievery is accompanied by divinely sanctioned genocide. After taking the land, 'You must utterly destroy them... show them no mercy' (Deut 7:2)."[75]*

Richard Heber Newton, an author from the late 1800s, writes:

> *"Thus the extermination of the Canaanites, for which the Hebrews pleaded long after the Divine order, and for which they had substantial warrant in Destiny's determination to rid the land of these corrupting tribes and make room for the noble life Israel was to develop, has been the stock argument of kings and soldiers for their bloody trade. Thus poor human consciences have been sorely hurt and troubled as men have read, in stories such as those of Jael and Sisera and Jacob and Esau, of act, which their better nature instinctively condemned."*[76]

It would also appear that elements of the Jewish doctrine are not original to the Jewish people, and elements were borrowed from other cultures--that notion effectively transforms their claim of exclusivity into mush. For example:

1) The idea of the devil isn't original to Judaism and the idea was borrowed from the doctrine of Zoroaster.[77]

2) The same applies to the ideas of Armageddon, Angels, Demons, and the resurrection of the dead. Those notions were introduced by the Zoroastrians and are not original to the Jewish people. Nor to the Christians and the Muslims.[78] It's believed Zoroaster's ideas were merged with Jewish beliefs during the enslavement of the Jews in Babylon, over 2 500 years ago.

3) The Sumerian myth of Gilgamesh is the inspiration behind the Garden of Eden.[79] The Persians and the Greeks also had their versions of the Garden before the Jewish people did. The Persians called it Heden and the Greeks named it Hesperidos.

4) The story of the great flood was recorded by the Sumerians, and several others, before the Hebrews documented it.[80]

Islam

Islam also believes that their Text is the true Words of God and all others are inaccurate. But Islam suffers from the same problems Judaism and Christianity do.

Prophet Mohammad never wrote what he thought or preached and the *Qur'an* was compiled near twenty years after he ascended into "The White Light". Initially, like the *Gospels*, the messages were communicated orally and *"then noted in fragmentary fashion on a number of material supports. When discrepancies in the recitations became highly apparent, they were collected together to form the Qur'an and published by the caliph Uthman."*[81] Consequently, all messages the caliph didn't approve were destroyed.[82]

Moreover, as Bart Ehrman points to in his book, *The Orthodox Corruption of Scripture: The effect of early Christological controversies on the text of the New Testament* (1997):

> *"The oldest passages that can be dated securely, however, are the inscriptions on the Dome of the Rock (called the Mosque of 'Umar) in Jerusalem, built in 691. These inscriptions are more in the Qur'anic style than they are Qur'anic, strictly speaking, since they do not coincide perfectly with the text we possess."*--(Page 71)

Now, I do not deny Mohammad or the idea that God sent a messenger to communicate with him. However, it's more than plausible that during the transmission of Mohammad's messages, by other people, to the caliph, information was forgotten, misquoted, or introduced. In addition, caliph Uthman was not Mohammad. It's possible that what he thought was an authentic message from Mohammad wasn't. Furthermore, he didn't have all the messages of Mohammad when he decided to compose the *Qur'an*.

I do not deny the *New Testament*, the *Old Testament*, or the *Qur'an*, and I have found God within all of them. But none of them hold a monopoly on the truth and none are absolute. For each to claim that they're the only religion with the absolute and uncorrupted truth doesn't relate to the evidence. And when a religion teaches their followers that only their Holy Text will provide salvation, they're attempting to create divisions amongst the people of the planet for political or economic reasons.

Jesus was very real, and if I could I would die for him. But that doesn't mean I would die for the New Testament. The New Testament is more so a product of the Roman Empire and what she transformed to become, the Holy Roman Catholic Church.

Although Godly ideas are present within the New Testament, as are the opposite, and I just can't give my Godly essence to that which isn't.

In that respect, I guess I was mistaken when I wrote that I wouldn't die for the New Testament. I would happily die for that which is God-oriented. To that extent, I would die for pieces of it.

I have no loyalty towards religion. I give all my loyalty to the truth, regardless of truth's origins. May the truth reside in the Old, the New, the Qur'an, the Vedas, or the Granth. May the truth reside in the poor, the meek, the ugly, or the mud. I am a servant of that which is forever. I am a servant of The One God and God's Principles.

People and Places

Most of the people (including giants) and the places found within most of the Holy Texts were probably real. Archaeological evidence cooperates and some of the places can be identified.

With respect to oddities like giants, researchers such as Michael A. Cremo and Richard L. Thompson are suggesting that the archaeological establishment has discovered the skeletal remains of human giants. They continue to assert that the discoveries are not popular because the findings contradict Darwin's Theory of Evolution. An assumption that isn't completely truthful--an idea briefly disclosed through the article "The Darwin Deception".

The *Bible* isn't the only that refers to giants. Cultures from around the world share stories of titans who once roamed the earth. The ancient Indians, Greeks, Chinese, Aboriginal Americans, and so on, all tell stories of giants. Some of these stories have taken on a fictional aura, and it's my belief that the stories were slowly embellished and given the characteristics common to a myth, but that wasn't how the tales were first told.

Most of the people and places within the Holy Texts were probably real, but I would suggest that the dialogue and the plot are fictional when the dialogue and plot advocate war, unnecessary terror, fear to gain obedience, murder, persecution, division, irrational conclusions, unneeded mediation like the vast Catholic administration, oppression, denial of the truth in other religions, and thieving motivations. In these cases, the dialogue and plot were most likely altered to motivate people to behave in a specific manner, and to help them view reality through a particular set of eyeglasses. Alterations to that effect stem from a political, personal, or economic agenda.

There are plausible fallacies coveted by religions. But that doesn't mean religions do not effort to nurture a God Consciousness. Through the understanding given above, study the spiritual path, the stories, the history, and the Texts prescribed by your religion. They are food for the soul and the cognitive condition. They will take you closer to the angelic.

Noah's Ark

Cultures from around the world claim that their ancestors experienced civilization-destroying deluges. Science also suggests that the world has experienced multiple large-scale floods. Fortunately, even though civilizations were annihilated, pockets of people survived their respective deluge.

After learning of the many floods the world has experienced, I'm inclined to believe that Noah and his family were one of those pockets. But this idea of Noah and his family as the only survivors is a political injection.

For example, the Sumer story of Ziusudra, the Indian story of Manu, the Greek story of Deucalion, and the Babylonian story of Utnapishtim all describe a man, who inspired by the heavens, built a boat so to survive a forthcoming flood. Some stories also detail a sea vessel capable of holding vast numbers of life. You might be inclined to think that all the tales are referring to one event, but the characteristics of each story are different from the next.

The idea, as with others, is presented as such, with Noah's family as the sole survivors, so to persuade people that the religion Noah's story stems from is associated with the only people in the world who were permitted to live by God. The idea is designed to manipulate the patron to believe those not of their house are inferior and false. Unfortunately, enough generations have recycled the lie that now a falsehood is taken as absolute and above rational discussion.

The Mayans too share a story of a deluge, and their story reveals another fascinating notion. The sacred book of the Maya, "the Popol Vuh", tells a story of a devastating flood in which the first beings were destroyed. The Mayans and many other ancient cultures from around the world, such as the Vedic culture, suggest that in the distance past, gods experimented to create the human being. Their first several creations were of an inferior character and eliminated. Eventually, the gods got it right.

Why Civilizations End

According to Eastern religious philosophy, the world continuously cycles through four ages. Before the introduction of each of the four eras, and before an age begins a decline, there happens a large-scale catastrophic event such as a flood that erases the majority of a civilization (people, culture, architecture, knowledge, technology, etc). The great flood spoken of by the Christians is a possible record of a civilization-erasing event.

Catastrophic world events set in motion by Universal principles created by God, take place before the introduction of an era to wipe clear what is. Each era gives birth to a new type of civilization, and for the new to fully be, in this case, the old must first be near-erased. The Mayans believed that human civilizations had already been wiped-out five times.

Each era produces a different type of civilization, as determined by the distance between humanity and God. In the first age, the people are closest to God and there exists only one religion. All people have God knowledge and all people are wardens of a God-Consciousness. But with each proceeding age, the people regress and move further from God, God knowledge, and a God-Consciousness. According to Sikh teachings, humanity is currently in the fourth era, the Age of Kali Yuga.

The forth epoch is said to be the darkest of all and furthest from the era of perfect existence. It is a time of dark influences and home to untruths. To one degree or another, almost all institutions facilitate falsehoods. That includes the culture and the intelligence filled and shaped by those institutions.

The four ages are: The Golden Age of Sat Yuga, the Silver Age of Trayta Yuga, the Brass Age of Dwaapar Yuga, and the Iron Age of Kali Yuga (also called the Age of Iron and the Age of Darkness).

"In the Golden Age of Sat Yuga, everyone embodied contentment and meditation; religion stood upon four feet. With mind and body, they sang of the Lord, and attained supreme peace. In their hearts was the spiritual wisdom of the Lord's Glorious Virtues. Their wealth was the spiritual wisdom of the Lord's Glorious Virtues; the Lord was their success, and to live as Gurmukh was

71

their glory. Inwardly and outwardly, they saw only the One Lord God; for them there was no other second. They centered their consciousness lovingly on the Lord, Har, Har. The Lord's Name was their companion, and in the Court of the Lord, they obtained honor. In the Golden Age of Sat Yuga, everyone embodied contentment and meditation; religion stood upon four feet. || 1 || *Then came the Silver Age of Trayta Yuga; men's minds were ruled by power, and they practiced celibacy and self-discipline. The fourth foot of religion dropped off, and three remained. Their hearts and minds were inflamed with anger. Their hearts and minds were filled with the horribly poisonous essence of anger. The kings fought their wars and obtained only pain. Their minds were afflicted with the illness of egotism, and their self-conceit and arrogance increased. If my Lord, Har, Har, shows His Mercy, my Lord and Master eradicates the poison by the Guru's Teachings and the Lord's Name. Then came the Silver Age of Trayta Yuga; men's minds were ruled by power, and they practiced celibacy and self-discipline.* || 2 || *The Brass Age of Dwaapar Yuga came, and people wandered in doubt. The Lord created the Gopis and Krishna. The penitents practiced penance, they offered sacred feasts and charity, and performed many rituals and religious rites. They performed many rituals and religious rites; two legs of religion dropped away, and only two legs remained. So many heroes waged great wars; in their egos they were ruined, and they ruined others as well. The Lord, Compassionate to the poor, led them to meet the Holy Guru. Meeting the True Guru, their filth is washed away. The Brass Age of Dwaapar Yuga came, and the people wandered in doubt. The Lord created the Gopis and Krishna.* || 3 || *The Lord ushered in the Dark Age, the Iron Age of Kali Yuga; three legs of religion were lost, and only the fourth leg remained intact. Acting in accordance with the Word of the Guru's Shabad, the medicine of the Lord's Name is obtained. Singing the Kirtan of the Lord's Praises, divine peace is obtained. The season of singing the Lord's Praise has arrived; the Lord's Name is glorified, and the Name of the Lord, Har, Har, grows in the field of the body. In the Dark Age of Kali Yuga, if one plants any other seed than the Name, all profit and capital is lost. Servant Nanak has found the*

72

Perfect Guru, who has revealed to him the Naam within his heart and mind. The Lord ushered in the Dark Age, the Iron Age of Kali Yuga; three legs of religion were lost, and only the fourth leg remained intact. || 4 || 4 || 11 ||"--(Sri Guru Granth Sahib Ji, ang 445-446 of 1430)

The term "Guru", used in the above passage, refers to God's Spirit and not a person. The name "Har, Har" is a name used to describe God. The Sikh Holy Text uses many different names to reference God.

This idea of the four ages is not exclusive to Sikhie thought. It's a very ancient idea that predates the oldest literature in the world, the Vedic literature, to over 12 000 years.

It's important to note that each age is accompanied by different planetary alignments. It's the change in the arrangement of the planets that stimulates catastrophic world events. In the Age of Sat Yug, in relation to the earth, Venus and Saturn play a much more dominant role. The symbol of Islam reflects that idea. The symbol is not of the Moon and Sun, but of Venus and Saturn.

Set to last approximately 24 000 years, there are two theories to what happens after this age. One suggests that the cycle starts again with Sat Yuga. Another theory suggests that the cycle doesn't begin again with Sat Yuga but instead descends after Kali Yuga passes.

The ancient Egyptians, Greeks, and Romans too valued this idea of the different epochs, with Greek philosophy hosting an additional age, the Age of Heroes. They even possessed maps of a world before the transition to the current age. On those maps, Antarctica isn't covered by ice and the above sea land mass is much larger. The Piri Reis Map and the Oronteus Finaeus Map, among others, are said to originate from those ancient maps.

Interestingly, the theory of the four ages provides an answer to a question mainstream historians are troubled by. They don't know or don't believe how the early civilizations, such as the Egyptians, gained the knowledge that allowed them to spontaneously civilize. They've even gone as far as to suggest that aliens were responsible for their advancement. But according to the ancient Egyptians, the knowledge required to civilize came from the previous ages, and it was knowledge that survived the transition from one era to another. The Sphinx is said to be from the previous age. Geologists have determined that the Sphinx is actually older than 10 000 years. They've determined that by examining the weathering the Sphinx has experienced. The examination determined that at one point, the Sphinx was exposed to heavy rain and it hasn't rained over the Sahara in over 10 000 years. If this is true, then the civilizations of this age are not as advanced as the civilizations of the past. We're playing catch-up. The supposition reminds me of a particular idea found in the Christian doctrine:

> *"What has been is what will be, and what has been done is what will be done; there is nothing new under the sun."*--(Ecclesiastes 1:4-11)

Other mysteries are also put into perspective when the theory of the four ages is applied to them. For example, the questions surrounding some of the megalithic structures found all over the world become less when considering the eras. It's possible that they were designed the sizes they were, in a previous age, to survive catastrophic world events brought forth by the transition from one epoch to another. Perhaps, the heavens inspired as they motivated Noah, but instead of a boat, instructions were provided to build huge stone structures.

Whereas ships such as Noah's stored life, the megalithic structures of the world might have stored knowledge. They just have to be looked at in the right light. For example, they give accurate astrological readings, their proportions are precise and mathematically arranged, they exhibit signs that advanced technology was used to make them, and they're built on what the Chinese call dragon lines and others call ley lines. It's also possible they contained written knowledge in the form of books and such, and that knowledge was retrieved after the catastrophic event. Perhaps, there's a storehouse of knowledge yet to be recovered.

Ships and megalithic buildings are not the only type of structures supposedly inspired by the heavens to survive an upcoming natural disaster. For example, in the second chapter of the *Vendidad*, a division of the Zoroastrian holy book *Avesta,* God warned the Persian King Yima, the son of Vivanghat, of an

74

upcoming natural disaster. God further instructed him to build underground cities and take shelter. Derinkuyu, the massive underground city discovered in Turkey, which can house as many as twenty thousand people, livestock, and the necessities required for tens-of-thousands of people to survive, is said to be one of the cities Yima built.

Elaborate underground cities, complexes, and tunnel systems are not all that strange. The ancient cultures from all over the world have one story or another detailing such things. For example, the Hopi and the Apache Indians believe that their ancestors once lived underground. Only after a great calamity, did they resurface.

In his book, *Weird America*, Jim Brandon shares the legend of the city underneath California's Death Valley called "Shin-Au-Av". The story originates from the Paiute Indians, and supposedly, in this mysterious underground complex, once lived an unknown race of people. The Sioux Indians also share an underground city story, in which one of their people, White Horse, accidentally found a city underneath the surface occupied by strange humans. These underground humans gave White Horse a mystical talisman capable of melting rocks.

There are numerous stories from all over the world detailing the existence of underground cities, complexes, and tunnels. The two most famous hidden underground cities are Agharta and Shambhala. Nazi Germany spent enormous amounts of money looking for the two, and it's suggested that they actually found Agharta. There, live tall, blonde, and blue-eyed people.

According to Eastern religious philosophy, the world continuously cycles through four ages, and humanity is currently in the fourth, the Age of Iron.

The Age of Iron is an age in which untruths dominate the world—provoked by the Universal force known as the Kali Yug, or the essence of what the Christians call the Devil.

The Age of Iron is the fourth age in a cycle of four, and unfortunately, it's an age considered the darkest. With the first depicted as the age of the pure.

Hell and Stuff

Some religious ideas, upon examination, appear to be man inspired. Ideas like "the Rapture". "The Rapture" is an idea created by a common man[83] and *"it is a fact that no Christian churches, congregations or fellowships that existed prior to 1830 proclaimed a 'rapture' doctrine."*[84] The idea of "the Rapture" was created by an individual by the name of John Darby of the Plymouth Brethren movement.[85]

If you're wondering what "the Rapture" is, according to the proponents of the theory, supposedly, there will come a day when only those who believe in Christ will receive salvation. In that moment, and within a flash, they'll be transported to heaven. The people remaining on the planet will endure some sort of trial and punishment.

Not surprisingly, ever since the invention of the idea, every generation who believed in "the Rapture" thought the phenomenon would happen in their lifetime.

"The Rapture" doesn't seem to be the only idea inspired by man. After inspection, ideas such as hell and the Devil also appear as constructs.[86]

It's very plausible that the Egyptian belief in the Underworld inspired the idea of hell. After which, the Hebrews borrowed the idea, fine-tuned it, and then transmitted it to the religions that followed. The Christians and the Muslims both stem from the Jewish tradition.

Interestingly, the belief in the underworld is an adaptation of the idea presented in the *Tablets of Thoth*. In which, the underworld is a place of light. The *Tablets of Thoth* are a better account of the Egyptian belief system than the nonsense mainstream archaeology has presented. Archaeologists prefer to depict the ancient Egyptians as superstitious and intellectually inferior people, but after a closer examination, they were far from ignorant.

However, through errors in transmission or intentional manipulation, the Jewish idea of hell is a place of darkness and ruled by the Devil. That said, none of the ancient Jewish literature reflects the popular idea of hell.[87]

The creation of the notion of hell was inspired by a desire to keep the masses scared, submissive, and obedient to the elite. In fear, people will do almost anything to relinquish that fear. The Greeks used similar devices. Thomas Thayer, in his book, *The Origins and History of the Doctrine of Endless*, writes:

> *"Any one at all familiar with the writings of the ancient Greeks or Romans, cannot fail to note how often it is admitted by them that the national religions were the inventions of the legislator and the priest, for the purpose of governing and restraining the common people...The object of this sacred fraud was to impress the minds of the multitude with religious awe, and command a more ready obedience of their part.... Of Course, in order to secure obedience, they were obliged to invent divine punishments for the disobedience of what they asserted to be divine law."*[88]

Unfortunately, the idea of hell has existed for so long that it's an idea taken as absolute and above debate--not to mention that every person is born with the abilities of a sinner and a saint. Why would God forever condemn what God knowingly made? Unless of course, God is truly cruel and created us only to see us burn and bleed, an idea that several religions facilitate.[89]

I do not deny the negative metaphysical consequences that spring from **sinful motion**. Nor do I deny heaven. I only challenge the popular notion of hell--a depiction that illustrates eternal damnation, eternal suffering, and eternal torture. It doesn't make sense for God to give the ability to sin and then forever condemn the human being for it.

The foremost consequence of sin is that it contaminates the aura a person emanates, and a polluted aura creates distance between the person and God's Spirit. God's Spirit is what liberates the person. The Spirit of God is brought to light in the last few articles of this section.

The popular idea of hell doesn't make sense. Neither does this idea of a cosmic battle between good and evil. Nor this creature called the Devil. The idea of a personified entity capable of challenging the power of God is a fictional account.

In view of the fact that God is the creator of all, why would God create an enemy or entity capable of equalling, challenging, and overthrowing? The idea of a cosmic battle and the idea of the Devil were ideas created to scare the people into obedience, to explain elements of nature not understood like the destructive power of the Universe, and to compliment and reinforce the false notion of hell. And "no", I don't think the Devil has the potential to overthrow The Creator of all. Everything is under the control of The Lord and Master. Moreover, The Great Architect dwells in all realms. If there is a hell, then God is the master there too.

The popular idea of the Devil tells a story of an entity who was once in the light of God, the perfect existence. But because of his jealousy of humanity, he rejected God and eventually left the light to destroy humanity. Two questions for those who believe--Is it possible for a negative like jealousy to exist in the light of God, and is God so weak that he can't prevent the Devil from interfering in human affairs? Jesus once said, as recorded in the *Gospel of Thomas*, *"Whoever believes that the All itself is deficient is (himself) completely deficient."*

Interestingly, the popular idea of the Devil doesn't seem to have a foundation within the *New Testament*.[90] Even in the *Old Testament*, Satan isn't made out to be as powerful as Satan is popularly known as.

Again, I do not deny the existence of the negative/destructive energy or the positive/creative energy within the Universe. However, the ideas of good and evil seem manmade and the phenomena those ideas attempt to describe were intentionally created by The Eternal.

In a sense, you can call the negative energy the Devil, however, without a sovereign will and similar to the idea of gravity, a Principle of the Universe. A Principle of the Universe created by The One Lord Master and under the authority of The One Lord Master.

The idea of burying the dead, so the corpse can be resurrected and collectively judged, is another concept rooted in popular misconception. This notion also limits the power of The Formless and confuses the mind's eye. The idea is confusing because it implies that God needs a blueprint to reconstitute the human condition. That interpretation suggests that God isn't as almighty as God truly is.

81

God doesn't need a bag of bones to create when with breath God created everything known and unknown. And if the body were meant to live forever, the design of the body would allow the body to live forever. That is the way of the Universe--that is the way of The Eternal.

The ways of The Eternal are not as mysterious as religions have presented them as. That is, after a person gains a firm understanding; an understanding buried underneath religious riddles and political spin that constantly misdirect the God seeker. As such, the person has little choice but to question before accepting a truth.

In some cases, the messages of the holy were changed. In other cases, religions misinterpreted the messages of the saintly or inserted their own selfish beliefs,[91] and the misinterpreted and/or inserted values have existed for so long that they've had time to mix with the facts, and along the way, they've managed to recruit passionate mullahs, clergymen, preachers, and priestesses.

82

When the Devil Attacks

Religions such as Christianity, Islam, and Sikhie suggest that as an individual progresses closer to understanding "that which was in the beginning and that which will be in the end", and on the verge of gaining intuitive spiritual wisdom, the essence of the Devil, if you will, attacks.

The universal law that constitutes the essence of the Devil, also referred to as the Kali Yug, intensifies its sway toward a person who is progressing toward a higher understanding. This essence attacks by influencing a person's thoughts, feelings, and metaphysical agents. The influence can, for example, distract the mind from progressing closer to The Eternal and spiritual wisdom, stress the mind into depression, or influence the metaphysical agents and beliefs of the ugly half of the mind's duality to create thoughts and actions. The ugly half is discussed in more detail in the upcoming chapter, and it is the part of the mind that houses the phenomena of lust, anger, attachment, selfish ego, and greed.

For this to be the case, then the law of the Devil must contain programming that enables it to sense a consciousness in progression. Moreover, with programming able to manipulate the vibrations of a person's cognitive agents. Keep in mind that everything in the Universe is in a constant state of vibration, and that includes thoughts and the metaphysical agents they originate from. The universal law of the Kali Yug must have the ability to manipulate the vibrations pertaining to the manner in which it attacks.

If an individual is under attack by this universal law, and if a person was attempting to move in a heavenly direction, the attack is a good indication that the individual is close to achieving the desired spiritual end. But remember, all is under the command of The Eternal Commander and Chief. That includes this universal law categorized as the Devil. Consider the influence of the Kali Yug as a test of your faith in The One Lord Master, administered by The One Lord Master, by way of a specific universal principle.

"Then Jesus was led by the Spirit into the wilderness to be tempted by the devil."--(Matthew 4:1)

Caught

When a moral crime is committed,
there is no escaping prison.
Caught by many, many method;
there is no outrunning consequence.
In the brain if not by body pain.
By Godly laws if not by cage.
Man's hand or The Divine's Hand,
subject is every soul that strays.

"If you do a thing openly or do it in secret, then surely Allah is Cognizant of all things."--(Qur'an 33:54)

Sin and Forgiveness

Several pages back, I mentioned the idea of the Catholic Confessional. The idea of the Confessional touches a very important concept. One common to most popular religions and an idea taught by the truly holy like Jesus--to daily request forgiveness for one's sins.

The fact of the matter is that we all sin for one reason or another, and we all house the cognitive agents that allow the person to sin. But what is a sin? Both the biblical and the historical usages deduced conclude that a sin is to prevent a person or the self from using or developing the better half of the mind's condition, and to ignore the divinity within the self or within others. The beautiful half of the mind's duality is highlighted in the following chapter, and it is the portion of the mind that houses the phenomena of compassion, humility, truth, and virtue.

Although the Confessional touches on a very important idea, I do not agree with their notion that an earthly intermediary is required to ask God for forgiveness. An individual can develop a personal relationship with The Eternal. Through focus of consciousness, an individual can directly ask The Lord to show pity and to forgive a person for their mistakes. Only then is an individual free of their sins.

All the holy individuals I've had the opportunity to learn from stressed the fact that there are temporary consequences after the body perishes. Fortunately, God isn't cruel and although the person is born with the programming to sin, God also created a universal law so to save the individual from the consequences of those discretions. With focus of consciousness, humbly ask The Fathomless to show pity and to forgive.

Even though The Eternal gave the person the ability to sin and prescribed consequences for it, The Formless also gave the human condition a remedy. The Eternal isn't cruel but loving.

Forgiving others is something to value as well, and it's as important as asking for forgiveness for the self.

> *"For if you forgive others their trespasses, your heavenly Father will also forgive you, but if you do not forgive others their*

trespasses, neither will your Father forgive your trespasses."-- (Matthew 6:14-15)

"I realized You, God Wise, to be progressive when I saw You at the birth of life, and found that You have ordained that actions and words should have consequences: bad for the bad, and good for the good. It shall be so through You excellence until the final turn of the creation."

Gathas: Song 8.5

What If: Karma and its Programming

The properties of the physical and the metaphysical differ. Is that because the metaphysical temporarily stays within this physical?

There is a reason for our uniqueness, for the complex metaphysical condition. In that, why would the human creature be any different and without purpose?

Perhaps, the purpose is to condition the metaphysical for the environment it enters after exiting the human body. Perhaps, the purpose of the person is to house the invisible condition--knowingly or unknowingly, developing it while living. Development determined by the type of information absorbed and the motions one engages in. When ascendance occurs, maybe, the type of energy developed will determine what like energy and environment it will naturally gravitate towards.

If the principles of reincarnation are true, then the shape or make-up of a person's energy might determine to where and what their energy will again manifest. Maybe, manifestation and energy attract each other. Maybe, certain types or shapes of energy naturally attract to specific manifestations. Maybe, it does matter what one becomes in life.

To navel gaze a little more, perhaps, the mind sleeps not only to give the body rest, and perhaps, the sleeping mind is sending communications of the days memories to the court of the Judge of Dharma (Karma). Perhaps, the Judge of Dharma evaluates those memories to determine tomorrow's Karma or a person's Karma after the body perishes, in turn, introducing positive or negative energy.

It could also be that the laws that govern Karma are within the person, and the human body doesn't send out communications but deliberates them within-- without the person's awareness.

How else could the court of Karma know everything about everyone? How else could the court of Karma justify administering judgment?

According to the suggestion, Karma not only plays a role in the type of daily experiences an individual encounters, Karma also prescribes what type of existence a person was born to. Genetics, inherited wealth, life experiences, innate spirituality, etc., are the result of a person's past life Karma. *"And even the very hairs of your head are all numbered."*--(Matthew 10:30) A person's constitution is predetermined and not random, and a person is born to a specific Karma. Although there might be a day-to-day deliberation, the deliberation and the action(s) that led to it, were predetermined.

That doesn't imply that Karma traps a person. A person can improve their Karma. You are not who you were, and you will not be who you are. It's an equation and you receive what you put it. Enter the better half of the mind into the formula and receive beautiful experiences--in this and the next. The most beautiful experience after the body falls is liberation from the cycle of life and death, and an existence in the perfect place--heaven. There, the "I" is one with The Great Architect. That said; The Formless scripts each living things Karma, and The Formless is the only that can rewrite what is written. The first step is to connect with God before Karma can be unscripted and scripted.

> *"So whatever you wish that others would do to you, do also to them, for this is the Law and the Prophets."*--(Matthew 7:12)

To one degree or another, most of the world's religions teach this idea of Karma--including the Jewish faith. The *Zohar* clearly details the concept. The only two popular dharmic institutions that do not explicitly teach their followers about the notion are Islam and Christianity. However, the idea of Karma can be identified within each of their doctrine.

"Be not deceived; God is not mocked: for whatsoever a man soweth, that shall he also reap."--(Galatians 6:7)

Freedom of Will/Choice

The belief in the freedom of indifference or the liberty of indifference is inaccurate. If a person does believe in this idea of indifference, it's because they haven't realized that environmental information, in combination with their intrinsic nature, creates their knowledge, wants, and beliefs. Knowledge, wants, and beliefs that inevitably lead to selections.

To be with a Freedom of Choice or Will, an individual would have to know everything possible or nothing at all. But to know nothing is almost impossible since the individual is born with innate units of information that influence. Moreover, the human condition will autonomously absorb information from its environments--it can't prevent itself. On the same note, it's impossible to know everything. It's impossible to know all because death limits the potential.

The nature of the person prevents the actualization of a Freedom of Will. That fact can only mean that choices are determined, and that by an individual's innate units and the information a person absorbs and the information a person doesn't--an individual can only make choices based on the information he or she has.

To restrict an individual's idea of freedom even further, within the framework presented above, a person can only choose what is available, accessible, and affordable. The same applies to the freedom to experience and to explore. A person can only experience and explore as far as their resources, options, beliefs, wants, and knowledge allow them to go.

Freedom of Choice or Freedom of Will is unattainable and the human condition's wants, beliefs, knowledge, and the thoughts they produce, are more determined than a person cares to admit. That doesn't mean that the choices a person makes do not decide a person's fate. However, the choices one has available to them and the choices the mind conceives are predetermined.

No person is outside the natural phenomenon that strips them of their Freedom of Will. All are slaves to the design of the human condition. The only true choice a person has is to operate fully determined or least determined.

Excluding the external determinants that influence, a person's level of determinism is aligned to the mastery of the mind or lack of it. In particular, the mastery of beliefs, wants, and the communications sent to the conscious and subconscious arenas.

To that effect, most deterministic is one who can't control the construction and flow of information within their mind. Half deterministic is one who can half control the construction and flow of information within their mind. And least deterministic is one who allows what information is constructed and what information enters the arena of thoughts and actions to the best of their abilities.

An individual least determined is like a pilot, and they understand cognitive cause and effect. Furthermore, they recognize how the person comes to be, they acknowledge why they want what they want, they recognize why they believe what they believe, and they understand what constitutes their being.

The difference... the difference between living determined and living enlightened.

Please keep in mind that mastery of the mind comes in stages and at given ages--determined by external information and internal influences (universal psycho kinetics). Nevertheless, all are capable and although genetics too are variables, more deterministic are environments. That's because they guide and teach. Capable they are of teaching me about me and guiding genes to be.

A sense of "nowness" is a greater freedom than a least determined mind. (A thought inspired by Osho the Wise).

93

Prophets and Politics

Unless touched by The Eternal, it's impossible to touch The Eternal. But touch those who The Formless touched and the path to The Great Architect will reveal itself. The essences of Jesus, Buddha, Nanak, Zarathushtra, Mohammad, etc. were one with The Lord. All are guides to the path. Pick any of them to lead, and through your mind's eye, attempt to touch.

However, some religions claim that their prophet is the only gateway to The Formless. For example, the Christians claim that Jesus is the shepherd, and Islam claims that Mohammad is the divine guide. Furthermore, they claim that all others are false. But, each of the holy from the many religions performed miracles, each revealed The Eternal, and countless people have utilized the spirit of each as a gateway to The Absolute. Accordingly, any of the holy can provide reception to The Celestial.

So, why are the holy on opposite ends?

After moving aside generations of political spin and digging through centuries of religious riddles, most religious institutions claim their prophet is the only for several reasons: 1) To empower the elite and their agenda. 2) To reinforce the religious institution's reputation as the only holder of divine truth. 3) To instil a sense of superiority within the followers. 4) And to motivate people to war and conquer.

It's much easier to convince a people to war against other people when they believe that the other represents a false prophet. It's much easier to convince a people to war if they feel that they're freeing another people from their false prophet. And it's much easier to convince a people to war if they feel that The Formless guides only them.

Some religions proclaim that their prophet is the only gateway to The Absolute, and it's my belief that politics played centuries ago, today, prevent those religions from acknowledging the others. But regardless of what those religious institutions may believe, regardless of the centuries that divide the baker and the cake, any and all of the prophets can provide a gateway. That is, so long as an individual's faith in The Absolute is true and steadfast.

A Rose is Still a Rose

Some believe that Jesus is God and all those who do not give God that name will burn in hell. I must ask--what about the billions who existed before the birth of Jesus, they never had an opportunity to know the name, did they all, by default, fall to hell?

I guess if God was cruel, that might be true.

The same people who believe the above also suggest, regardless of a person's character, that by simply accepting the name "Jesus", an individual will automatically enter heaven after death. However, that isn't what the *New Testament* advocates. If only the entrance to heaven was that easy to pass through. The passage below proposes that a corrupt character is too big to fit through the gateway to heaven--no matter if he accepted the name of Jesus.

> *"For it is easier for a camel to go through a needle's eye, than for a rich man to enter into the kingdom of God."*--(Luke 18:25)

It isn't the name a person gives The One Divine or the image a person chooses to see The One in, it's a person's state of consciousness that determines existence after death, life on earth, and love for The One. Besides, a rose is still a rose no matter the name it's given.

If a person wishes to name The Eternal Energy, Jesus, well, that's all good. But the fact of the matter is that if another chooses to call that same Eternal Energy another name such as Allah, Ahura Mazda, Gobind, Jehovah, or Waheguru, that too is all good. They're all attempting to describe The One.

Again, it's not the name but an individual's state of consciousness that determines their life, their death, and their love for The One. It's the only thing that truly makes universal sense.

The Word

When a person hears the word "God", their mind will naturally bring forth the images and the associations they absorbed to represent the idea of God. It's similar to what happens when a person hears the word "apple", and that phenomenon can limit a person's awareness.

I don't have the knowledge to give a full account of God, but I prefer to think of the One as Timeless, Formless, Fathomless, Limitless, and The Primal Energy everything known and unknown is contained within. Such a description resonates with my soul. The others limit my understanding of The Great Architect. I just can't confine "God" to an image of an old man, with a white beard, floating amongst the clouds, constantly wrestling the devil, and daily administering punishment; or a young man with dusty-blonde hair and blue eyes; or for that matter, a God represented by a particular colour, form, or gender.

Any attribute that limits the power of The Creator isn't truth. Nor is any attribute that isn't virtuous, loving, and pure. God is not cruel. God is much more.

The Holy Text of the Sikh people, *Sri Guru Granth Sahib*, inspired the brief and incomplete description of The Lord expressed above. The account given by that Holy Text doesn't seem to limit The Great Architect.

I do not wish to endeavour to give an account of God beyond what I've already written. I just don't have the mental capacity to undertake that particular task, and all my efforts will fall short. But, the Sikh prayer, "Mool Mantra", provides a compelling account of The Eternal.

Mool Mantra: *Ik Onkar. Sat Naam. Kartaa Purakh. Nirbhau. Nirvair. Akaal Moorat. Ajooni Saibhang. Gurprasad.*

"Ik--There is ONE (Ik) reality, the origin and the source of everything. The creation did not come out of nothing. When there was nothing, there was ONE, Ik.

Onkar--When Ik becomes the creative principal it becomes Onkar. Onkar manifests as visible and invisible phenomenon. The creative

97

principle is not separated from the created--it is present throughout the creation in an unbroken form, 'kaar'.

Sat Naam--The sustaining principle of Ik is Satnaam, the True Name.

Kartaa Purakh--Ik Onkar is Creator and Doer (Kartaa) of everything.

Nirbhau--That Ik Onkar is devoid of any fear, because there is nothing but itself.

Nirvair--That Ik Onkar is devoid of any enmity, because there is nothing but itself.

Akaal Moorat--That Ik Onkar is beyond Time (Akaal) and yet existing.

Ajooni--That Ik Onkar does not condense and come into any birth. All the phenomenon of birth and death of forms are within it.

Saibhang--That Ik Onkar exists on its own, by its own. It is not caused by anything before it or beyond it.

Gurprasaad--That Ik Onkar expresses itself through God-Manifest, known as Sat Guru. Through the Lord's grace and mercy (Prasaad) this happens. "--(Source: http://www.sikhiwiki.org/index.php/Mool_Mantar)

"True In The Primal Beginning. True Throughout The Ages. True Here And Now. O Nanak, Forever And Ever True. ||1|| By thinking, He cannot be reduced to thought, even by thinking hundreds of thousands of times. "--(Sri Guru Granth Sahib Ji, ang 1 of 1430)

Timeless, Formless, Fathomless

"Ik Onkar". The symbol above represents the idea of the One God worshipped by all: No matter the name given, a rose is still a rose regardless.

Man in God's Image?

If man is in God's image, is that image the body or something else?

In the Holy Text, *Sri Guru Granth Sahib Ji*, ang (page) 318 of 1430, translation to English by Singh Sahib Sant Singh Khalsa, MD, it reads:

> *"You are the One, pervading in all; you are contained in all. You are diffused throughout and permeating all places and interspaces; you are known to be deep within the hearts of all beings."*

The same sort of message is within the *Qur'an*, the *Gathas*, the *Vedas*, and the others. That idea naturally leads a person to think that the image of The Formless isn't the physical but the inner light within the person.

You be the judge. Is it that with the potential of immortality, the invisible within, or is it the body, which is designed and guaranteed to perish?

God is Within

The Eternal Commander and Chief created all, and in doing so, The Eternal infused the essence that is God within everything that exists. Without that essence, there would be nothing to support the Universe and all its principles and inhabitants, including the human condition's breath of life. For that reason, every single human being is equal to another.

This idea of God within the individual troubles one of the most popular religions, and I think it's because they don't fully understand the idea. It seems as if the belief of God within the human condition implies to Christendom that the person is God. However, that isn't the case. God is within all creation and separate from (onto thyself). But without the essence of The Primal Void, nothing can exist.

Not surprisingly, the above notion wasn't foreign to the Christian's before Constantine created the *New Testament,* especially among the Gnostics. But Constantine didn't like the idea. Such ideas would discourage the Christian from invading other people's places, taking their possessions, murdering them, and stealing their land to expand the Roman Empire. To hurt another is to hurt the God within them, and why would anyone who appreciates the idea endeavour to hurt another knowing The Primal Void also feels it?

> *"Jesus said, 'If they say to you -where did you come from? Say to them--we came from the light, the place where the light came into being on its own accord and established [itself] and became manifest through their image. If they say to you--is it you? Say-- we are its children, we are the elect of the Living Father. If they ask you--what is the sign of your father in you? Say to them--it is movement and repose.'"*--(Gospel of Thomas)

Countless saints have spoken of God in such a manner. Great philosophers such as Hermes Trismegistus and Aristotle too expressed the idea. The All-Mind is within all minds.

They also articulated that to discover The Light within (God's essence) is one of the highest life purposes. But be warned, the task is extremely difficult and mastery of meditation, of internal vibrations, and of the mind are a prerequisite. The end goal is to allow the identical self to consume the self.

The purpose is to allow The Light (God) within to govern the mind and body so to eventually merge with The Supreme Light. When The Light within is discovered, nurtured, and finally merged with The Supreme Light, an individual is considered one with The Primal Void and The Primal Void is considered one with the individual. It's been said by countless saints, when an individual does reach that state of being, there is no difference between the two.

When an individual does achieve such a state of being, they are no longer subject to the principles of the Universe that govern life and death. The potential for immortality is the individual's but not immortality of the physical. Death can be overcome.

So, search for The Light within, God is closer to you than some popular religions have propagated. As Jesus expressed, the true church is within the body fortress.

God is within and there's a concentration of the God essence within the heart and the heart chakra. The Egyptians believed so strongly in the idea that when they would mummify a dead body, they would throw away the brain and pay overwhelming attention to the heart. The heart had more value than the brain.

The Egyptians were not and are not the only people who give the heart and the heart chakra importance. Most other spiritual paths that utilize the chakras of the human condition also accommodate the same understanding.

> "Wherever I look, I see that One Lord alone. Deep within each and every heart, He Himself is contained. ||1||Pause||"--(Sri Guru Granth Sahib Ji, ang 387 of 1430)

The person is a body fortress and within is The Great Architect. Not only that, the human body is constituted by divine instruments such as the Ida and Pingali, and these tools are capable of connecting the person with God. The second volume to *Secrets of Religion* explains the idea.

The Eternal Commander and Chief created all, and in doing so, The Eternal infused the essence that is God within everything that exists. Without that essence, there would be nothing to support the Universe and all its principles and inhabitants.

The popular religions believe that all creation sprung from God's "Word", God's "Breath", or God separated Thy Self. They're all claiming that creation came from a singular point. If that's true then nothing within the Universe can be without elements from that singular point of creation. Thus, God must also be within. But please don't be mistaken, there is only One God and no person could ever be The Great-Giver.

<u>Jesus' Sacrifice</u>

Christianity pushes the idea that Jesus sacrificed himself on the cross for the world's sins, and so the world could continue to exist. A quick question--If Jesus died for the world's sins, why has humanity continued to sin? The idea doesn't truly make sense.

I believe that Jesus was persecuted on the cross, but I don't believe he sacrificed himself for the world's sins. If anything, he sacrificed himself for the Divine Truth he was attempting to communicate to those who had strayed. Besides, The Almighty is powerful enough to erase the world's sins without having to engage in a blood sacrifice and all the drama surrounding it.

Not only do I not fully accept the idea of Jesus and the world's sins, I also do not believe in the notion of a blood sacrifice. Christianity proclaims that Jesus was the last blood sacrifice and no other blood sacrifices were now required. By Christianity claiming that Jesus was the last blood sacrifice, and as such, no other blood sacrifices were required to appease The Celestial, suggests the foundation of Christianity is a human blood sacrifice.

It's more than plausible that the idea of Jesus as the last blood sacrifice came to be so to persuade the Pagans that no more blood sacrifices were necessary to appease The Celestial, and to make Christianity more attractive to the Pagans. Constantine desired to make the Empire Christian, but a large portion of the Empire was Pagan. Being the good politician that the Roman Emperor was, he understood that to persuade the Pagans to adopt Christianity, the Christian doctrine must be a little Pagan.

This article doesn't deny that Jesus foresaw his death or the impact his death would have. Nor does it deny that he didn't know what he was doing or that he could perform miracles such as raising the dead, healing the sick, and feeding a few hundred people with a single loaf of bread. The Divine touched Jesus and he was capable of the impossible. I'm only presenting reasonable questions.

Eggs and the Easter Bunny

Paganism, Paganism, Paganism... One of the greatest challenges of the Christian Nation is to relieve itself of the injected Pagan doctrine.

The more I read of Christianity and the more I relate it to its origins, plausibility begins to lose its validity when discussing if Pagan ideas have infiltrated the House of Jesus.

For example, the celebration, Easter, appears to cater to Pagan elements and those elements are not *Scriptural*. The *Bible* mentions nothing of the popular elements surrounding Easter. Lent, eggs, egg hunts, bunnies, etc. aren't anywhere in the Holy Book. Furthermore, the original apostles and early *New Testament* Churches didn't even acknowledge Easter.

The elements of Easter seem to stem from the worship of the Sumerian goddess Ishtar. "Ishtar" is pronounced as you would the word "Easter" and, like many others the world over, Ishtar is said to have resurrected.

Ishtar is the goddess of fertility, and people worship her in the spring since spring symbolizes the renewal of life. With time, an association evolved between eggs and fertility, and eggs were eventually incorporated into the worship of Ishtar.

Now, the Bunny doesn't come from the same place the egg does. Bunnies appear to be a remnant of the festival of Eostre, a great Northern goddess-- signified by the hare. The hare was transformed into the rabbit and then engulfed by Easter. *"The hare, the symbol of fertility in ancient Egypt... Its place has been taken by the Easter rabbit".*--(Encyclopaedia Britannica, 1991 ed., Vol. 4, pg. 333)

The challenge of Christianity is to filter out the Pagan elements that so long ago made Christianity their home. They seem to have taken residence when the Roman Emperor was converting the Empire into a Christian dominion. Again, to appease the large Pagan population not willing to forget their Pagan roots, and to quell any potential civil conflict with the Pagans, the Empire compromised and allowed Pagan elements to join the newly consolidated Christian doctrine.

The other popular religions of the world also support some form of Paganism. The different doctrines of Paganism were the standard before the emergence of monolithic religions and the initial converts to the popular religions were Pagan. They did not completely leave behind their original beliefs when they converted. Jewish Cabbalism and Islamic Sufism are excellent examples of the mergers.

Although the elements of Easter are most likely Pagan in origin, and eggs and bunnies have nothing to do with Jesus, that doesn't deny the resurrection of Jesus. Jesus and individuals of such distinction are able to bend and break the laws of the Universe. And let's not forget who his ally was, the Spirit. The Spirit is capable of every miraculous happening you can imagine.

Is Jesus the Sun god?

Some theorists have suggested that there was no Jesus and Jesus is a reference to the Pagan Sun god. Furthermore, they deny the people who witnessed Jesus such as the disciples, and they propose that each represents a constellation of the Zodiac. However, these theorists have reached the wrong conclusion. Their assumption that the *Bible* refers to the Pagan Sun god and such things as the Zodiac are correct, but Jesus and the disciples were real and they existed.

Astrology was very big with the Pagans and they did worship the planets within the solar system. They believed each planet was a conscious entity able to assistance them. To placate the Pagans, during Constantine's conversion of the Roman Empire to a Christian dominion, he merged Christian personalities with those the Pagans worshiped, and each personality represents two notions. The term "Jesus", in the *Bible*, represents the actual Jesus to the Christians, but to the Pagans, the term refers to the Sun god. The same applies to the disciples. However, there might have been more or less than twelve, and the designation of that number might be so to correlate to the number of signs in the Zodiac.

The merger of the two doctrines was only a success because Constantine compromised the Christian philosophy, but to say that Jesus didn't exist because of the amalgamation isn't accurate, and many, many historical happenings support the fact that he lived on this planet.

110

If Jesus was a Mortal Man

Excluding Christianity, most religions believe that God has no family--no wife, no sister, no mother, no brother, no father, no daughter, and no son. God was the only in the beginning and God will be the only in the end. So, why did this idea of Jesus as God's progeny come about?

Jesus was a Divine spirit but I think this idea of Jesus as something more than a human being is a plausible political injection.

The depiction of Jesus as a mortal man, who sacrificed himself in the struggle for the greater good and for a better world, could potentially inspire others to bring about positive social change or resist tyranny as he did. The Roman Emperor didn't want to inspire anyone strong enough to resist to ask the questions--If Jesus could do it, why can't I; if a mortal man can do it, why can't I? The Emperor didn't want Jesus promoted as a revolutionary martyr. That idea could inspire a socially conscious revolution. For that reason, Constantine moulded an image of Jesus as more than human.

That all said, Jesus was God, in the sense that the identical self had consumed the self. Jesus had shed the illusion of reality and merged with The Great Architect. However, that potential is in every human being, and many saints have accomplished the same. Now, that doesn't mean Jesus was immortal, he was mortal with the same physical fragility as every other human being.

The idea of "turning the other cheek" was also plausibly changed when the *New Testament* was consolidated. There must be more to the idea.

There were times when Jesus didn't turn the other cheek. For instance, Jesus didn't like the immoral idea of the Jewish people collecting taxes in the place God was worshipped. Instead of turning the other cheek, Jesus, like a champion, rushed the Jewish Temple and flipped a few tables. By his actions, Jesus communicated that there are times when it isn't righteous to turn the other cheek.

By indoctrinating the idea of "turning the other cheek" without the idea further explained, the Emperor and the Catholic Church were able to potentially subdue any effective resistance before an effective resistance even came into existence. Christian Lions turned into political sheep by the Roman Empire.

Fortunate for religion but unfortunate for the woman and man, every generation is born unaware of what is and what was, and generations born to tomorrow won't know of the past if the past isn't taught.

If No Jesus

If no Abraham,
if no Moses,
if no Jesus,
if no Mohammad,
if no Nanak,
would there be the One?

If no Gospels,
if no Qur'an,
if no Gathas,
if no Granth,
would there be God?

Why do we allow for the divisions when in the beginning and the end, there is only One? We reinforce the divisions because each believes that they're the only with the truth. Each believes that their prophet or their book is the absolute.

But most prophets and most holy books have much in common. Each taught and teaches the person to live through the better half of the mind's duality and to live a God conscious life.

Just as there are commonalities, there are also differences, and people believe in either reincarnation, the Garden, or the Day of Judgement. Disconnected from all the arguments, all the arguments are valid. Conversely, there is an absolute just as there is for everything scientifically known about the Universe. I don't know what that absolute is, and when you sit down and give it thought, it doesn't really matter. The commonalities prescribe one mean and all ends are reached by travelling the same road and stepping on the same stone--all ends are reached by developing the beautiful half of the mind and the soul. The beautiful half of the mind gives live to such happenings as humility, compassion, love, a desire for truth, and so on. Whatever the fixed is, each who travels that road and steps on that stone is subject to the absolute, regardless of whether they were aware or unaware of that truth.

So, let it be reincarnation, the Garden, or the Day of Judgement. It doesn't matter. The true Christian, the true Sikh, the true Hebrew, and the true Muslim all hold hands, travel the same road, and step on the same stone.

Stepping Stone

Judgement Day, **Liberation**, or the perfect secular existence, all require the same from the faithful. A heavenly incarnation, a righteous resurrection, or a return to the Garden, all ends are reached by guiding the growth of the consciousness and the soul. Regardless of what you believe, all ends are reached by conquering the parts of the mind that block the divine and corrupt the human potential--all ends are reached by allowing the beautiful mind to hold the soul of an angel.

The two foremost variables, the soul of an angel and the beautiful (the better half of the mind, where live love, compassion, truth, humility, self-restraint, virtue, kindness, etc.), with them as your comrades, the outcome after death is most favourable. No matter if a person believes in some sort of individual judgement after the body falls, or if they believe that all will rise together and stand before The Court of the Lord.

So, stand on opposite ends but respect the outlook of the other. Please appreciate that the journey is one and we all step on the same stone.

How to Choose Heaven

The One Lord and Master is "The Great Architect". The One Lord and Master protects those who connect. The One Lord and Master is the commander of life and death. The One Lord and Master shields the servant.

The One Lord and Master fashioned the Universe. The One Lord and Master scripted the known and unknown principles. The One Lord and Master wrote the metaphysical and the physical verse. The One Lord and Master created everything as a subject of an equation regardless of the averse.

None can escape the above facts. None are above the Divine Act. None are able to refract. None are exempt from The Celestial Contract.

So, let it be Judgement, Hell, Heaven, or the other options, all are chosen. Enter the better half of the mind into the equation and choose Heaven. Oh, and of course, with focus of consciousness, forever love The Divine Captain.

The Creator of the Universal Chieftain rendered Universal Principles as sovereign equations, and The Creator of the Universal Chieftain decided to sit outside while playing "the great game" from within.

<u>Prayer</u>

Most religions have prayers for their members to recite. For the most part, the prayers of each are different. In specific, the words within the prayers are unalike. However, the purposes of the words in the prayers appear to be the same.

The words within all prayers are designed to assist the mind's eye focus towards The Light within and The Supreme Light. But to recite the words without understanding the words, and to recite the words without focusing the consciousness towards the reality they were designed to reveal, any and all prayers are potentially barren.

Moreover, if the prayers are properly recited in the language they were written, while focusing the consciousness, specific vibrations will be produced and they will invoke subtle mystical experiences. That is, if the prayer was written by a person who understood the power of vibrations and able to organize the appropriate words to create the appropriate vibrations.

Although the words within the many religious prayers may differ, it appears the objectives of each are similar. And although some religious institutions like to claim that only their prayers have value, the truth is that all prayers are precious.

For some people, praying once a day is difficult. So, when I discovered that the devote Muslim prays five times a day--dawn, noon, afternoon, sunset, and night, I was astonished. An admirable quality it is and a routine other faiths should consider adopting.

To learn from the different religions should be encouraged. But the political machine that is religion doesn't benefit when that happens. Their power and influence would be threatened if the people of the planet didn't maintain the divisions.

My suspicion is, beyond the religious riddles hidden underneath political truths, it is the consciousness through which I can comprehend. It's the only method that truly makes sense. A gift locked until one comes to understand.

Over and Out

All day in confession and still a person may not be forgiven.

Every sunrise and sunset in prayer and still a person's prayers may fall silent.

A lifetime reading the *Bible* or the *Qur'an* and still a person may fail Judgement.

From birth to death repeating the *Guru Granth* and still a person may not be liberated.

Please appreciate that it isn't an act but a person's state of awareness.

The connection between the person and The Supreme Light can be made but only through the right frequency. It's similar to tuning into the right frequency on a Citizens Band Radio, and a person's awareness must be dialled in to send and receive.

Death

Every religion I delved into prescribed reactions to actions of ethical and moral compromise. That is, if a person doesn't rise above them. The journey after the body falls can be difficult or smooth. Good karma brings about an easy journey. Bad karma manifests obstacles--"hell" is home to several of those obstructions.

Life after death is a journey. The Greeks and the Egyptians symbolized that journey with a boat, and Sikhie thought refers to an ocean of some sort. The Abrahamic religions too believe in an afterlife expedition, for example, hell, purgatory, or heaven.

If a person isn't ready for the journey after the "I" disconnects from the body, an individual might not understand it. Perhaps, they'll accidentally fear it and not embrace the natural transition.

All the religions I studied expressed that life after death was a reality, and how an individual lives affects that existence. They further suggest that it is better to live through the beautiful half of the mind. That half helps an individual prepare for the next, and that half offers a much more favourable passage than that provided by the selfish. The beautiful half of the mind is where the notions of compassion, love, and truth exist, and the selfish half of the mind is where the ugly characteristics of a person such as anger, lust, greed, and attachment reside.

So, I guess it truly doesn't matter how much capital one banks. It doesn't matter the name of the occupation to which one is chained. It doesn't matter what type of clothes one wears. It doesn't matter how fancy a cake an individual can bake. If our corporeal were immortal, then it would matter, but since death is an absolute, it doesn't make long-term sense to give long-term value to a stage short and interim.

Forget for a moment where you be. Lean back, close your eyes and walk with the holy. There, take the time to compare the ideas of morality and sin, and breathing and ascendance. Egoless, let the soul determine what is best to secure happiness... in this and the next.

124

To feel another's hurt - To love the Maker and the world - To remember.

To move in kindness - To give with compassion - To practice forgiveness.

To be God Conscious

God's Name

One idea of utmost importance, communicated by many, many Holy Books, but most explicitly in the Sikh Holy Text, *Sri Guru Granth Sahib,* is the value of God's Name.

The Name is salvation. The Name is nirvana. The Name is the cure for all ailments. The Name is so because it activates the unstruck sound current of "The Word" within the person. When The Word is active within the body, it unlocks salvation, it unlocks nirvana, and it unlocks the all-in-one medicine.

The idea of The Word (God's Word) is within most doctrine, and The Word, as with The Name, is a unique vibration that supports the constitution of everything that exists. Without that support, nothing, excluding God, can be.

Vibrations produced through sound can alter the metaphysical and physical. The vibrations of sound have power. Using a candle flame, Swami Murugesu's *Flame Experiment* demonstrated the impact of certain words on the material. With specific sounds, the color of the flame would change, as would its overall presence.

The power of The Word is indescribable and from The Word comes all creation, within all creation is The Word, and in The Word all merge.

> *"When the body dies, where does the soul go? It is absorbed into the untouched, unstruck melody of the Word of the Shabad."*--(Sri Guru Granth Sahib Ji, ang 327 of 1430)

> *"The Unstruck Sound-current of the Shabad, the Word of God, vibrates in the Court of the Lord."*--(Sri Guru Granth Sahib Ji, ang 1137 of 1430)

> *"In the beginning was the Word, and the Word was with God, and the Word was God."*--(John 1:1)

Sri Guru Granth Sahib also emphasizes that only God reveals God's Name. In specific, God Spiritually-Manifest. God is said to be Unmanifest and Manifest, and "Sat Guru" (True Guru) is the term used by *Sri Guru Granth Sahib* to identify the second. To connect with Sat Guru, a person should meditate towards, sincerely beg The Lord, and do their best to be a God Conscious Citizen. A description of a God Conscious Citizen is in the upcoming chapter. Such a person is in a state of being ideal for a celestial experience. Their person produces a resonance Sat Guru favours. Without it, God Manifest doesn't approach.

> *"Without serving the True Guru, the Naam is not obtained. The Naam is the True profit in this world. || 6 || True is His Will, beauteous and pleasing through the Word of the Shabad. The Panch Shabad, the five primal sounds, vibrate and resonate."*-- (Sri Guru Granth Sahib Ji, ang 1059 of 1430)

The idea of Sat Guru is in almost all religions and in the *New Testament*, the *Old Testament*, and the *Qur'an*, the terms the Spirit, the Holy Spirit, and the Spirit of God signify the same as Sat Guru.

> *"Flesh gives birth to flesh, but the Spirit gives birth to spirit. You should not be surprised at my saying, 'You must be born again.' The wind blows wherever it pleases. You hear its sound, but you cannot tell where it comes from or where it is going. So it is with everyone born of the Spirit."*--(John 3:6-8)

> *"Do not cast me away from Your presence, and do not take Your Holy Spirit from me."*--(Psalm 51:11)

> *"When he and his servant arrived at Gibeah, a procession of prophets met him; the Spirit of God came powerfully upon him, and he joined in their prophesying."*--(Samuel 10:10)

> *"Therein descend angels and the Spirit by the command of their Lord--with every matter."*--(Qur'an 97:5)

Sometimes, this notion of God Manifest isn't so easy to identify, and as author Alexander Smith suggests in his book, *The Holiest Lie Ever: Glorified by Myths, Mysticism, Symbolism, Rituals and Traditions,* the symbols of the dove and fire, at times, refer to the Holy Spirit. These symbols can be found in a multitude of religions including those of the ancient Greeks, the Romans, the Druids, the Egyptians, the Incas, the Hindus, the Buddhists, and the Celts, who claim their Salic Laws were guided by Sat Guru. The Celts termed the Holy Spirit, Salo Ghost.

Sri Guru Granth Sahib firmly believes that meditation on The Name, through thoughtfulness or repetition, has greater spiritual merit than any visit to a sacred place of pilgrimage, material object, prayer, posture, or Holy Book. The most exalted offering a person can make to The Eternal is The Name.

Meditation on The Name is important and not just solitary reflection. The practice within a society of saints is highly valued by *Sri Guru Granth Sahib*. If you ever, by God's Grace, encounter a true society of saints, take the time to meditate with them. If you can, selflessly serve them. A true saint is immersed in The Name, and a true saint is the outcome of the self consumed by the identical-self. Tell me--is there any earthy person more worthy of selfless service?

> *"In the Saadh Sangat, the Company of the Holy, the Lord of the World is understood."*--(Sri Guru Granth Sahib Ji, ang 1156 of 1430)

The true saints are above the duality of the mind--they are egoless and absorbed in The Word. For them, the world exists, and by their angelic efforts, such as celestial meditation, the world continues to exist. If God has favourites, they are it, and among them, Sat Guru is.

The Name is salvation. The Name is nirvana. The Name is the cure for all ailments. The Name is so because it activates the unstruck sound current of "The Word" within the person.

"He gives life and causes death, and to Him you shall be brought back."-- (Qur'an 10:56)

The Foremost Trinity

The three foremost objectives in the attempt to discover The Great Architect are:

> To connect with the Holy Spirit.

> To connect with The Word.

> To connect with The Name.

Rebirth

After spending time reviewing religious doctrine, I was blessed with a revelation, the awareness of God's Spirit.

A common understanding there is, God is Unmanifest and God is also Spiritually-Manifest. The Great Architect is in all creation, and simultaneously, unto the self--interacting with God Unmanifest. God Spiritually-Manifest is most commonly referred to as the Holy Spirit.

In relation to the person, God's Spirit is a teacher--the all-knowing and always truthful Professor. A lecture conducted by the Spirit will reveal reality's true nature. But only when the student is ready, will the teacher appear.

> *"At that time Jesus, full of joy through the Holy Spirit, said, 'I praise you, Father, Lord of heaven and earth, because you have hidden these things from the wise and learned, and revealed them to little children. Yes, Father, for this was your good pleasure.'"*-- (Luke 10:21)

> *"For God has revealed them to us by his Spirit. The Spirit searches all things, even the deep things of God."*--(1 Corinthians 2:10)

> *"We have not received the spirit of the world but the Spirit who is from God, that we may understand what God has freely given us."*--(1 Corinthians 2:12)

The influence and instruction of the Holy Spirit is necessary to understand The Great Architect. Without it, no person will truly grasp the wonders of God. If a person were to forget all religion and entrust strictly in the Holy Spirit, they would gain enlightenment. The Holy Spirit taught all the prophets, even the wise Hermes Trismegistus was a student. He referred to God Manifest as Poimandres, the Great Dragon. For that reason, religions have much in common. The source was the same. The differences are earthly assertions.

The Perfect Guru teaches the person and no individual can truly understand the nature of reality without the Immaculate Professor. But God's Spirit can do much more for the God seeker. The Holy Ghost can purify and unite.

133

In an instant, the Holy Spirit can transform the beliefs, thoughts, and wants of a person. That includes the neural pathways that facilitate them. The Spirit of God has the ability to bring a change to the body and mind, and that change is in harmony with the expectations of the Holy Spirit.

> *"For the sinful nature desires what is contrary to the Spirit, and the Spirit what is contrary to the sinful nature. They are in conflict with each other, so that you are not to do whatever you want."*-- (Galatians 5:17)

> *"But the fruit of the Spirit is love, joy, peace, patience, kindness, goodness, faithfulness."*--(Galatians 5:22)

The Spirit of God cleanses by reprogramming the person to function through the better half of the mind and under the influence of the soul. The nature of the beautiful half and the soul are highlighted in the upcoming chapter.

> *"He saved us, not because of righteous things we had done, but because of his mercy. He saved us through the washing of rebirth and renewal by the Holy Spirit."*--(Titus 3:5)

The Spirit of God has the power to set right the manner in which a person operates, and a purification is a requirement before an individual can unite with The Formless. Consider this. The person is like a drop of water dyed with purple color, in a body of the clearest water. Until the purple color is removed from the droplet, it will never truly merge into the whole. The Holy Spirit eliminates that color. Without God's Spirit, regardless of how thin the color might get, the person will never merge.

God Unmanifest introduces God Spiritually-Manifest to the person, and the second unites the individual with God-Unmanifest. That is, after a rebirth.

An individual may have mastered their chakras, learned how to manipulate the principles of the Universe so to perform miracles, or accumulated all the wealth the planet has to offer, but without the Holy Spirit, they will never merge with The Great Architect. The Holy Spirit is the only able to merge a person with God, and that by activating God's Word. The Word is within every individual, and The Word's nature liberates the true self and provides a link to The Eternal.

I Salute the Spirit

The person comes into the world innocent, with little knowledge of the reality cast into, and an individual learns of the world from the givers of information such as governments, movies, music, corporations, the family tree, and religions.

Regrettably, all of them have the potential to, purposely or accidentally, communicate inaccurate knowledge, and a person can grow to live a life governed by an untruthful value system.

The consciousness can be misinformed and an individual can live a lie without knowing it. But there is a teacher forever truthful and who is eternally incorruptible. This giver of knowledge will never purposely or unknowingly mislead the person. I forever salute the Spirit.

Chapter 1
Part III: Sikhie and Hinduism

So far, we've predominantly discussed the Abrahamic religions, but they aren't the only that were infiltrated by political motivations. The remainder of the chapter will examine the Sikh and the Hindu doctrines, and a few of the elements that raise reasonable questions.

Infiltrated by Self-Interest

> *"Quite a large number of office bearers of the present SGPC are communists, virtual atheists and drunks. There is nothing religious about them and their only achievement is that they have alienated all the traditional bulwarks such as the Udasis, Nirmalas, Sewa-Panthis and Nihungs. A revolution against the present massive corruption, where political workers have been appointed as priests and religious propagandists, and no literature worth the name in any language has been printed in any language, is long overdue."*--(Dr. Trilochan Singh, *The Turban and the Sword of the Sikhs*, pg. 328)

The above statement becomes an observable fact when you visit the major Gurudawaras (Sikh places of meditation and worship) in Punjab--in particular, when you visit Harmunder Sahib (Golden Temple).

Harmunder Sahib is the holiest place of the Sikh people, but it was infiltrated by self-interest and selfish people, and the committee empowered to govern Gurudawaras, the SGPC, allowed it to happen. When they hire priests, servants, guards, etc, they don't care about the qualifications of a person as much as what that person can do for them. Nepotism is also a factor. These unqualified people are corrupting the Sikh people, and they were instrumental in ushering in the darkness that now clouds the Sikh nation.

Furthermore, holy places such as the Golden Temple, for all intents and purposes, were transformed into businesses. For example, at Harmunder Sahib, there are dozens of donation boxes within the complex and most of them have *Guru Granth Sahib Ji* placed above them. They've placed multiple copies of the Sikh Holy Text so to justify placing a donation box underneath it. They are exploiting the Eleventh Guru, and tragically, the corruption at the Golden Temple will persuade people to consider the entire place as corrupt. The truth and purity of the Harmunder Sahib will be overlooked.

Not surprisingly, the Golden Temple generates more revenue than the State of Punjab--the Sikhs are extremely generous people. (Punjab is the State the Golden Temple resides in). However, the revenue gathered isn't reinvested to strengthen the Sikh nation. If it were, the conditions of the Sikh people, within

Punjab, would not be so horrid. The money is said to instead support a specific political family.

This political family hold positions of authority within the S.G.P.C, and members of this clan were in favour of the 1984 attack on the Golden Temple. Could it be that they supported the attack so to have specific members of the S.G.P.C, of that time, eliminated? Could it be that they eliminated them so to take their positions of power and the finances attached?

The Golden Temple isn't the only that was hijacked, as were multiple other Gurudawaras. The only way to determine which is corrupt is to experience for the self. However, some are easily identifiable, and those that operate under a license of private ownership should be criticized. The profits they generate are not reinvested. Profits line the pockets of the owners of the business. Multiple Gurudawaras in a small area, for no justifiable reason, should also be examined. I've visited cities where there are several Gurudawaras a few blocks apart from each other, and each appeared to be competing with the others. Which of them was infiltrated, I'm not sure, and the only way to gauge the corruption is to experience for the self.

Tables and Chairs in Gurudawaras

I'm sure most people in Canada have heard of the "tables and chairs" controversy that happened several years back, involving the Sikh community. But I don't think most fully understand the unnecessary drama that was the actual cause of the conflict. ("Sikh" is pronounced as the word "sick" is, and the word means "to learn").

The conflict was more between competing groups vying for leadership roles within the Sikh places of worship and meditation (Gurudawaras). In the process, they attempted to change the definition of a Sikh by introducing the terms "fundamentalist" and "moderate".

However, there can never be a moderate or a fundamentalist. There can only be Sikh. To attach the word "moderate" to the word "Sikh" is to change the definition. To attach the word "fundamentalist" to the word "Sikh" is to imply that there is a division. The Sikh philosophy and the Sikh way of life are not like water, which can be poured into any shape a person chooses and drunk. The Sikh philosophy and the Sikh way of life are like a big boulder--solid. Either you are or you are not.

The unnecessary drama over tables and chairs was actually about control of the lucrative finances generated by Gurudawaras. One group who wanted control exploited a misunderstood notion--an idea that challenged the accepted practice in the contemporary Gurudawaras.

One side pushed the idea that all people who eat within a Gurudawara should sit on the floor to eat--as the ancient Sikhs did. Even the ancient kings were not exempt. The other side didn't agree.

The idea of sitting on the ground was practiced to promote equality amongst the high and low of society, in a time when there weren't enough chairs for all to sit on. But in the contemporary world, there are enough chairs on which to sit. If all the people are sitting on a chair, what does it matter, the idea of equality is still preserved.

Regardless, those who were interested in money weren't interested in debating doctrine and reasonably reaching a conclusion. They exploited the idea of equality to position their interests.

Unfortunately, the conflict has led to the creation of new types of Gurudawaras, and also a new revenue stream for those who were looking for monetary gain. I guess they accomplished their mission.

An Appearance--the 5 Ks

Some religions have evolved to believe that an appearance determines a person's Godliness. For example, the religion of the Sikhs relentlessly promotes this idea. However, the idea is inaccurate. An image doesn't determine a person's metaphysical worth.

Contemporary Sikhism holds the belief that until an individual undergoes Amrit (the Sikh baptism ritual) and adorns the 5 Ks, he or she isn't a member of the House of Nanak. Moreover, the Sikh Code of Conduct--*the Reht Maryada*--reinforces this belief. However, this belief actually contradicts the teachings of Guru Nanak, the father of Sikhie, and *the Reht Maryada* does more to mislead the Sikh nation than it does to lead it.

The 5 Ks are: Unshorn Hair (Kesh), Wooden Comb (Kanga), Steel Bracelet (Kara), Undergarment (Kachhera), and Sword (kirpan).

1) Unshorn Hair symbolizes dignity, represents submission to nature's realm, and enhances a person's potential to connect with the Primal Energy that pervades through all.

2) Wooden Comb symbolizes mental, physical, and spiritual cleanliness.

3) Steel Bracelet symbolizes the unbreakable bond with God, and serves as a reminder to allow the five weapons (truth, contentment, humility, compassion, and love) to govern one's actions.

4) Undergarment symbolizes modesty, athletic prowess, and mental control. In particular, mental control over one of the five thieves--lust. The energy of the orgasm is to be harness and not abused.

5) Sword symbolizes the duty to protect the weak, to protect dharma, to protect the holy of all religions, to protect the self, and to control the mind. The sword should be used as a shield. Accordingly, the thieves of the mind that persuade the mind to do the opposite must be controlled. The five thieves are anger, attachment, greed, lust, and the selfish ego.

Guru Nanak didn't believe that an outer appearance or a material object determined a person's potential or capability to develop a relationship with the One. Guru Nanak believed that a person's state of awareness determined his or her devotion. Guru Nanak also believed that an appearance or a material object didn't reflect a person's state of awareness. Or for that matter, their belief about the self, other people, life, death, the natural, **the absolute**, and the built world.

Moreover, an appearance or a tangible item as a prerequisite creates a religion of exclusion and divides religion from religion, and people from people. Guru Nanak believed that the only force that separates a person from another person is the condition of the mind. Either a person is God Conscious or a person isn't. More important, Guru Nanak worked to unite religions and not further divide religions. Remember the Guru's proverb, *there is no Hindu and there is no Muslim.* All that said, in 1699, Guru Gobind, the 10th manifestation of Nanak, introduced the 5 Ks.

The intention behind the 5 Ks could not have been to contradict what Guru Nanak Ji believed. The outer appearance of a person doesn't determine a person's Godliness. **Guru Gobind Singh** himself agreed to that statement. In his book, *Bachittar Natak*, he writes, *"Let people go wherever they like, they will find that God is not to be found in the outer garbs."* However, what Guru Gobind Singh Ji did do was create the Khalsa, an armed branch of Sikhie. As a member of the Khalsa, an individual is asked to accept Amrit and adorn the 5 Ks. In essence, Guru Gobind attached the idea of a soldier to Guru Nanak's idea of a saint and designed the saint-soldier, with the introduction of the Khalsa.

Guru Gobind Singh considered the Khalsa the army of God. The purposes of the Khalsa are to free the weak from the grips of all tyrannical powers, to defend dharma, to protect the holy, and to selflessly serve humanity.

The Khalsa wasn't an overnight creation, and the Sikh leadership began employing an informal armed force soon after the Mughal Empire adopted a radical viewpoint. By the time of the 10th Guru, the conditions of India were so intolerable that a formal armed force was required so to defend against the tyranny of the Mughals. Moreover, Guru Gobind understood that the Imperial Army was one of the world's most effective, and to defend against an

144

organized army, the defenders must also organize. Along that line of thought, the 5 Ks create a unique and unifying identity among the members of the Khalsa.

The 5 Ks were also designed to instil a sense of confidence. Most of the 5 Ks-- the sword, the long hair, and the beard--were adorned by the elite, the holy, and the warrior-class of India. What I'm suggesting is that they were accepted symbols of power, elite-hood, and dignity. An appearance socially recognized to carry respect and power has the potential to uplift the psyche of the individual who appears as such. By all accounts, the first wave of people who joined the Khalsa were from the lower classes, and according to Sikh historian, John Malcolm, they were in need of a mental boost (*Sketch of the Sikhs*, pg. 149).

Similarly, Gobind was attempting to make replicas of himself; mentally, spiritually, and physically. He writes in Bachittar Natak, *"The Khalsa is my image and I reside in The Khalsa."*

Furthermore, the 5 Ks symbolize hope. Hope for the people of India. Guru Gobind expected every member of the Khalsa to defend those in need of defence. In addition, if a people expect a certain type of behaviour from a person, that individual is more likely to behave in the manner he or she is expected to behave in. The 5 Ks not only create an expectation for, but also an expectation from.

Guru Gobind did not contradict Guru Nanak and an appearance doesn't determine an individual's love for and from God. The introduction of an appearance was for other reasons than to determine who is God oriented and who is not.

As for the Sikh Code of Conduct, *the Reht Maryada*, the Shromani Gurudwara Parbandhak Committee (S.G.P.C) created it between the years 1931 and 1950, and it articulates that a person must undergo Amrit and adorn the 5 Ks.

It's important to remember that the construction of the Sikh Code of Conduct began under British occupation. We really don't know the intentions behind the design of *the Reht Maryada*. However, the colonial intentions of the British are well known, and they were not in the business of nurturing and enhancing cultures. They were in the business of corrupting them to control them.

It can also be argued that *the Reht Maryada* has no spiritual or temporal authority over the Sikh nation because the Sikh Guru bestowed no authority upon it. The Guru gave *Guru Granth Sahib Ji* to measure the self against. If the Guru believed that the people required additional guidelines, I'm sure the Guru would've incorporated them into *Guru Granth Sahib Ji*. After the creation of the Khalsa, and before he ascended, Guru Gobind Singh Ji had ample time to fuse the 5 Ks into the character of the Eleventh and final Guru. However, he decided not to.

It should be mentioned that only a small number of people finalized the Code of Conduct and prominent Sikh individuals refused to attend the delegation that applied the final stamp--individuals such as Sant Gurbachin, Baba Nand Singh, and Baba Atter Singh. The argument can be made that they didn't attend because they were true to the Eleventh Guru, and that truth interfered with the agenda of the people who created *the Reht Maryada*.

For the most part, the prerequisites within *the Reht Maryada* are aligned to the ideas within *Guru Granth Sahib Ji*. However, a few passages read inaccurately when compared to the ideas within the *Granth*. Some ideas read like rituals. Some ideas create inequality. Some ideas create exclusion. Some ideas detract from Nanak's message. And some ideas mislead. Inaccuracies were mixed together with Sikh truths and presented as wholly accurate, for example:

1) *The Reht Maryada* implies that there is no truth in other religions but that isn't what Guru Nanak suggested. Guru Nanak believed that there's truth in all religions. The Sikhs owe their allegiance to the truth before anything that indicates otherwise. The truth and not religion should be the guide.

The Reht Maryada also instructs the Sikhs to disregard the holy places of other religions and only visit Sikhie holy places. Again, the founder of Sikhie didn't believe that. Guru Nanak visited the holy places of other religions. Guru Nanak also believed that holy places were inconsequential in a person's search for God. He believed that a person's state of mind is what truly matters, regardless if at Mecca, if at Amritsar, or if at Jerusalem.

146

What's more, the Guru included the words of those not of the Sikh faith in *Guru Granth Sahib Ji*, and after reading the ideas attributed to Buddha, Jesus, Mohammad, and Nanak, I discovered that they had much in common. Maybe, God's words aren't exclusive to only one of the God sent.

Excerpt from *the Reht Maryada*

> *"(d) ...Not owning up or regarding as hallowed any place other than the Guru's place--such, for instance, as sacred spots or places of pilgrimage of other faiths. Not believing in or according any authority to...the Vedas, the Shastras, the Gayatri (Hindu scriptural prayer unto the sun), the Gita, the Quran, the Bible, etc... However, the study of the books of other faiths for general self-education is admissible."--(Shiromani Gurdwara Parbandhak Committee [S.G.P.C]. Sikh Reht Maryada: The Code of Sikh Conduct and Convention. Amritsar, Punjab, India: Gold Offset Press, 1994. Chapter X, Article XVI.)*

2) *The Reht Maryada* implies that the baptized Sikh is the highest creed of Sikh. An idea that every other baptized Sikh seems to reinforce. However, that creates a type of caste system within Sikhie, between the non-baptized Sikh and the baptized Sikh. The Sikh Guru worked to abolish manmade ideas that create inequality and divide a person from a person. The Sikh Guru believed that all are equal, no matter their title, creed, or appearance.

Excerpts from *the Reht Maryada*

> *"(q) Only an Amritdhari (baptized) Sikh man or woman, who faithfully observes the discipline ordained for the baptized Sikhs, can enter the hallowed enclosures of the takhts. Ardas for and on behalf of any Sikh or non-Sikh, except a fallen or punished Sikh, can be offered at takhts."--(Ibid., Chapter IV, Article V.)*

> *"(c) Only a Sikh (Amritdhari, as defined in the Reht Maryada) man or woman, is entitled to be in attendance of the Guru Granth during the congregational session."--(Ibid., Chapter VI, Article VII.)*

147

3) *The Reht Maryada* appears fixated with an individual's appearance. Again, Nanak stressed that it's a person's state of awareness that determines their loyalty to him, Sat Guru, and The Absolute, not what an individual wore or didn't wear, or how they looked or didn't look.

Excerpts from t*he Reht Maryada*

> *"(k) Piercing of nose or ears for wearing ornaments is forbidden for Sikh men and women."--(Ibid., Chapter X, Article XVI.)*

> *"(s) It is not proper for a Sikh woman to wear veil or keep her face hidden by veil or cover."--(Ibid., Chapter X, Article XVI.)*

> *"(q) The following individuals shall be liable to chastisement involving automatic boycott:*
> *(3) One who dyes his beard."--(Ibid., Chapter XIII, Article XXIV.)*

4) *The Reht Maryada* is overshadowed by an anti-Islamic tone but the Khalsa isn't anti-Islam. The Khalsa is anti-tyranny. We must not forget that during the time of Guru Gobind, Muslims fought alongside the Sikhs, and during the reign of Maharaja Ranjit Singh, Muslims were employed by the Sikh nation-state.

5) And *the Reht Maryada* contradicts itself. It implies that other religions are inferior, and on the same note, it asks a Sikh not to hurt the sentiments of the people from other religions. But by implying that other religions are inferior, doesn't *the Reht Maryada* disrespect the people of other religions? Again, Nanak believed that there is truth in all religions, regardless if *the Reht Maryad*a suggests otherwise.

Excerpt from *the Reht Maryada*

> *"(e)The Khalsa should maintain its distinctiveness among the professors of different religions of the world, but should not hurt the sentiments of any person professing another religion."--(Ibid., Chapter X, Article XVI.)*

Sections of *the Reht Maryada* are not aligned with the teachings of the Sikh Holy Text, and we should ask ourselves, why would a group of people take it upon themselves to create a constitution-like article?

I believe that the agenda of the S.G.P.C. was to legitimize their authority, and for that reason, they decided to take it upon themselves to create a code of conduct. Just as a constitution can empower a government, the S.G.P.C. thought that a code of conduct would do the same for them.

Now, I don't think the existence of the S.G.P.C. would be a problem if they were uplifting the Sikh nation. However, they don't fulfill their obligations.

If they had fulfilled their obligations, why is Punjab in shambles? Why is the Sikh nation close to defeat? Punjab is plagued by illiteracy, inequality, injustice, liquor, hunger, poverty, etc. and the Sikh leadership does little to clean up the mess.

If they had fulfilled their obligations, why do so many Sikhs not understand what a Sikhie is?

If they had fulfilled their obligations, why haven't they challenged the tyrants of the world? Guru Gobind's Khalsa was conceived to bring peace, equality, and justice to the planet. Why isn't the S.G.P.C. helping to realize his vision?

In the end, *Guru Granth Sahib Ji* is the highest Sikh authority and not *the Reht Maryada*. In actuality, *the Reht Maryada* has absolutely no authority because no authority was bestowed upon it.

It's more than plausible that the intentions behind *the Reht Maryada* were to ward off the Hindu incursion into Sikhie. For decades before the creation of the Code of Conduct, the Hindus attempted to absorb Sikhie. No matter, the code still contains anti-Sikh rhetoric.

Contemporary Sikhism holds the belief that until an individual undergoes Amrit (the Sikh baptism ritual) and adorns the 5 Ks, he or she isn't a member of the House of Nanak. Moreover, the Sikh Code of Conduct--*the Reht Maryada*--reinforces this belief. However, the belief actually contradicts the teachings of Guru Nanak, the father of Sikhie, and *the Reht Maryada* does more to mislead the Sikh nation than it does to lead it.

"Says Kabeer, those humble people become pure - they become Khalsa - who know the Lord's loving devotional worship.||4||3||"- -Ang 655 of 1430, Sri Guru Granth Sahib Ji

The Khalsa

There is no moderate and there is no fundamentalist. The only distinction within Sikhie is that between those who've accepted Amrit, baptism and initiation into the Khalsa, and those Sikhs who haven't. Regardless, all are of the same house and all are of the House of Nanak.

As for those who've accepted Amrit and entered the mystic Khalsa, more is asked of them than those Sikhs who haven't. In addition to accepting the Five Ks, the individual should understand that the Khalsa is an armed union designed by Guru Gobind Singh for the purpose of defending against all tyrannical powers, protecting dharma, and protecting the holy of all religions, without taking anything in return. To that effect, each member of the Khalsa should be physically and spiritually prepared to battle, and mentally prepared to give his or her life for the cause. Death is a companion of the Singh (a member of the Khalsa). There is no compromising. Puran Singh, a renowned Sikh academic, writes in his book, *Spirit of the Sikh*:

> *"Death, apparent death, is embraced by The Khalsa as no lover ever embraced his sweetheart. The Khalsa dies like the dashing waves of the sea, creating in the wake of its death millions more like itself. The life-breath of The Khalsa thus is losing its apparent life to gain its life everlasting."*

> *"In the ideal of The Khalsa, one can see the Ideal spirit of the passionate love of death for the sale of life as is seen in the Bushido of the Samurai of Old Japan. In that fervour of Yamoto, the physical life turns all into a little moth flickering its wings in infinite impatience to die. Death is the bride of the brave."*

Max Arthur McAuliffe, in his book, *The Sikh Religion: Volume 1*, writes, *"...no superiority of the enemies in number, no shot, no shell, can make his heart quail, since his Amrit (baptism) binds him to fight single-handed against millions."* Rightfully so, the tyrannical forces of the world have always been as strong as a million giants and those who were brave enough to stand against like the Biblical "David". Only without fear and only with a will to sacrifice everything worldly, can the giants be defeated.

It's also important to understand that not only is the Khalsa a community of warriors, the Khalsa is a community of saints. Each member should be humble, kind, gentle, loving, peaceful, fearless, forgiving, God-oriented, communally aware, soft-spoken, rational, truthful, mentally disciplined, knowledgeable, poetic, worldly, and detached from the self and **Maya**. The Khalsa only unsheathes the sword as a shield and not for secular gain. Puran Singh once wrote:

> *"Once it is said The Khalsa occupied the throne of Delhi when the Mughal Emperor submitted and acknowledged the power of The Khalsa, the leader Jassa Singh said--'Ah! The Khalsa is atit (untouched by Maya). What has it to do with thrones'--and gave the throne back to the Mughals."*

> *"No one need be afraid of The Khalsa of Guru Gobind Singh, that it would ever think of seeking the bones of material objects. The eyes of The Khalsa are fixed heavenward."*

As dictated by Guru Gobind Singh to the great Sikh scholar, Bhai Nand Lal Goya, Goya writes in his book, *Tankhahnama*:

> *"The Khalsa is he who protects the poor, who destroys the wicked, who recites the Name, who fights the enemy, who concentrates his mind on the Name, who is detached from all other ties, who rides the horse, who fights every day, who bears arms, who promotes dharam, and who dies for his faith."*

The famous Sikh historian, Rattan Singh Bhangu, writes in his book, *Pracheen Panth Prakash*, the following about the creation of the Khalsa. *"The perfect Guru the Tenth created the Khalsa Panth in this manner, so that they must wage a war against oppression."*

154

Guru Gobind Ji further describes the Khalsa as *"he is whose heart burns unflickering the Lamp of Naam, day and night, know him the Khalsa, the pure!"* As recorded in Puran Singh's book.

That connection to the essence of God, is the reason the Khalsa's history is full of Singhs able to overcome incredible odds and perform superhuman deeds akin to that performed by **Banda Singh, Deep Singh, Hari Singh**, and **Jassa Singh**. As the Jedi draws power from the Force, the Singh draws power from the Lamp of **Naam** (The Primal energy that pervades within all known and unknown).

An 18th century Muslim historian, and an enemy of the Sikhs, Qazi Nur Mohammad, once wrote of the Khalsa and the Khalsa's spirit:

"Do not call the Sikhs dogs, because they are lions and are courageous like lions in the battlefield. How can a hero, who roars like a lion be called a dog? Like lions they spread terror in the field of battle. If you wish to learn the art of war, come face to face with them in the battlefield. They will demonstrate it to you in such a way that one and all will shower praise on them. If you wish to learn the science of war, O swordsman, learn from them. They advance at the enemy boldly and come back safely after action. Understand; Singh is their title, a form of address for them. It is not justice to call them dogs; if you do not know Hindustani language, then understand that the word 'Singh' means a lion.

Truly, they are lion in battle, and at times of peace, they surpass in generosity. When they take the Indian sword in their hands they traverse the country from Hind to Sind. None can stand against them in battle, howsoever strong he may be. When they handle the spear, they shatter the ranks of the enemy. When they raise the heads of their spears towards the sky, they would pierce even through the Caucasus. When they adjust the strings of the bows, place in them the enemy killing arrows and pull the strings to their ears, the body of the enemy begins to shiver with fear. When their battle axes fall upon the armour of their opponents, their armour becomes their coffin.

The body of every one of them is like a piece of rock and in physical grandeur every one of them is more than fifty men. It is said that Behram Gore killed wild asses and lions. But if he were to come face to face with them even he would bow before them. Besides usual arms, they take their guns in hand and come into the field of action jumping and roaring like lions and raise slogans. They tear asunder the chests of many and shed blood of several in the dust. You say that musket is a weapon of ancient times, it appears to be a creation of these dogs rather than Socrates. Who else than these dogs can be adept in the use of muskets. They do not bother even if there are innumerable muskets. To the right and the left, in front and towards the back, they go on operating hundreds of muskets angrily and regularly.

...Besides their fighting, listen to one more thing in which they excel all other warriors. They never kill a coward who is running away from the battlefield. They do not rob a woman of her wealth or ornaments whether she is rich or a servant. There is no adultery among these dogs, nor are they mischievous people... There is no thief amongst these dogs, nor is there amongst them any mean people. They do not keep company with adulaters'... Now that you have familiarised yourself with the behaviour of the Sikhs, you may also know something about their country. They have divided Punjab amongst themselves and have bestowed it upon every young and old. "--Jang Namah (1765)

Jang Namah is an eye-witness account of Ahmed Shah Durrani's 1764 invasion of Punjab. Commissioned by Ahmed Shah, the author naturally compromises objectivity when describing events and the people of the nation they invaded. When reading his work, it becomes evident that Nur Mohammed had a strong prejudice against Sikhs. He refers to them with such names as dogs, dirty idolaters, fire worshippers, etc. Nevertheless, even with his biases, he was unable to prevent himself from glorifying the Khalsa and the Khalsa's members.

Qazi Nur Mohammad also recorded the event that saw Baba Gurbakhsh Singh Shaheed, and 30 Sikhs, battle 30, 000 Afghanies in an attempt to protect the

Holiest Place of Worship, The Golden Temple. Guru Gobind Singh Ji truly transformed the weak of India into titans.

The true Singh, a replica of Gobind, is able to harness Naam because those who serve the Khalsa serve God. The Khalsa is a union of the Pure--the spiritually liberated, and sanctioned by The Lord for the purpose of ushering in the "Kingdom of God." What the Singhs have come to call the Khalsa Raj, in which God, truth, equality, justice, freedom, and righteousness prevail. It is said that so long as the Singh is true to the principles of the Khalsa, God will protect the Singh. However, The Great Architect is quick to abandon those who forget that it was not man who strengthened and willed the creation of the Khalsa, but The Eternal. The primary reason the Sikhs lost their empire. Ranjit's sons and those around them did not practice sainthood.

According to author, Narain Singh, in his book, *Guru Gobind Singh Re-told*, a year prior to the creation of the Khalsa, Guru Gobind retreated into the Naina Devi Hills to meditate. He was troubled by the fact that he was forced to resort to violence to combat violence. He was fully aware that violence was an evil that destroyed human values and an idea that contradicted the core teachings of Sikhie--love and non-violence. However, the Mughals, in their quest to convert all of India to Islam, unleashed hell on the people of India. Only those who unsheathed the sword were able to retain their non-Islamic identity. Guru Gobind unsheathed out of necessity, and even though each battle resulted in his victory, he was fully aware that violence was unbecoming. For that reason, he retreated into the hills where he meditated and requested guidance from The Eternal.

Gobind eventually united with The Formless One, and after his union, Gobind proclaimed, as written in his book, *Bachittar Natak*:

> *"The Lord has sent me into the world for the purpose of spreading Dharma. He said to me, 'Go and spread Dharma (righteousness) everywhere, seize and smash the evil doers.' Know ye holy men, I have come solely for the purpose of bringing about Dharma, saving holy men and completely uprooting wicked men."*

After his union, Guru Gobind created the Khalsa and initiated the quest to restore the conditions of an honourable existence. Conceived as a champion of dharma, the Khalsa was sanctioned by The Eternal to unsheathe but only in the face of extreme evil, and when peace is useless.

From my understanding, the only distinction within Sikhie is that between those who've accepted Amrit, baptism and initiation into the Khalsa, and those Sikhs who haven't. Regardless, all are of the same house and all are of the House of Nanak.

"The needy alone deserve to be endowed with rare gifts, what is the use of empowering those who are already powerful. The House of Nanak is known for its compassion and generosity, and known as the saviour and protector of the poor."--Rattan Singh Bhangu, *Pracheen Panth Prakash* (1810)

3HO: How a Denomination Can Come to Be

Religious denominations come into existence for three principle reasons: To challenge the distortions a religious institution might be perpetrating, to fulfill a personal agenda, or to corrupt the beliefs of the root religion from which it stems.

When researching the faith of the Sikh people, a particular idea became allusively apparent. A faith can be attacked by the creation of a sub-faith that takes the same name but practice differently. Typically, these sub-faiths maintain the majority of the practices and beliefs from where they stem, but they'll also introduce practices and doctrine that distort or weaken the faith the sub-faith adopted.

When researching the faith of the Sikh people, I discovered a group who believe they're practicing the Sikh faith accurately, but when compared to the ancient Sikhs, they aren't. The name of the group is "3HO".

3HO, created by Yogi Bhajan in 1969, is an organization that distorts the faith it attempts to stem from. Although they adhere to the majority of the Sikhie philosophy, they also adhere to doctrine that is very much unSikh. Ideas that contradict what the Guru taught. They've also managed to pacify one of the greatest achievements of the Guru. They've managed to pacify the saintly fighting force known as the Khalsa. The 3HO have managed to, amongst their members, separate the soldier from the saint and effectively bury the saint-soldier in the pages of the history their writing. (The saint-soldier is another name for a member of the Khalsa).

The place Yogi Bhajan chose to begin his crusade, New Mexico, was a place with no prominent Sikhs to challenge his distorted teachings. The Westerner didn't know any better than what Yogi Bhajan taught. By the time the Sikhs discovered the anti-Sikh practices and doctrine, the Westerners who had adopted Yogi Bhajan's distortion were so far conditioned that they consider and considered the actual Sikhie philosophy, practices, and history as that which is inaccurate. To get a brief idea of the differences between Sikhie and 3HO, take a look at the video titled, *"The 3HO and how they differ from real Sikhism"*. [92]

Some of the inaccurate practices and beliefs 3HO Sikhs accommodate are:

159

•Tantric Yoga (Tantric Sex Yoga).[93]

•Numerology.[94]

•Priesthood--a type of caste system.[95]

•Idolatry.[96]

•Tantra Mantra.[97]

•The placement of Hindu idols and pictures around *Guru Granth Sahib Ji*, as witnessed and articulated by Kim Douglas in her book, *High Desert: A Journey of Survival and Hope*. In the Ashram, she writes, *"I liked the high ceiling, the tall open windows, the four white walls featuring a photo of Yogi Bhajan and several colorful and dramatic pictures of the gods and goddesses from the Hindu scriptures".*[98]

•Yoga. Yoga isn't a foremost practice of the Sikhs, and Guru Nanak prescribed contemplation of "The True Name" through prayer, logic, song, mediation, and virtuous deeds as the ultimate means to connect with The Primal Energy. Within the Sikh doctrine, all other practices are secondary.

> *"Bhai Gurdas (One of the greatest Sikh writers from ancient times) tells us that Guru Nanak met all Yogis, Siddhas, and those who claimed to be avatars of ancient Yogis, and through debate and spiritual influence he scored victory over them and made them submit to his ideology."*[99]

These practices, and the beliefs they facilitate, are more so Hindu in nature, and practices the Sikh Guru worked to eliminate from the popular culture's collective consciousness. As reported by Time Magazine, in an article titled, Yogi Bhajan's Synthetic Sikhism (Sept. 5th, 1977). *"The kind of Sikhism preached by Bhajan...is far different from that practiced by 10 million Indians."* The article continues to read. *"High Priest Jaswant Singh, a leader of the Sikhs in eastern India...last week denounced Bhajan's claims. He and his council professed to be 'shocked' at Bhajan's 'fantastic theories.' Yoga, Tantrism and the 'sexual practices' taught by Bhajan, the council declared, are 'forbidden and immoral.'"*

Not only do the 3HO stray from Sikhie, it's been suggested that the organization is a cult. *"Kamalla Rose Kaur, another former member of Yogi Bhajan's 3HO, said a light switched on when she was researching religious groups, 'Hey, we're acting a lot like a cult.'"*[100]

160

At this point, I think it's very important to mention that ever since Sikhie grew in prominence, the elite Hindu has attempted to incorporate it into the Hindu system, distort the true nature of Sikhie, or destroy it completely. After Indian Independence (after the elite Hindu took control of India), their attempts only intensified. At the time of Bhajan's appearance in America, the Indian Government was engaged in strategic warfare against the Sikhs. The creation of the 3HO Sikhs is an attempt at Hinduizing the Sikh faith in the West before actual Sikhie took root with the Westerner.

Interesting enough, Yogi Bhajan is alleged to be a sleeper asset for the Indian Intelligence Agency and the R.S.S.[101] The R.S.S. is a Hindu terrorist organization and both groups have actively worked to accomplish the goals mentioned above.

While researching the 3HO, I found the book, *Sikhism and Tantric Yoga*, by Dr. Trilochan, a very useful analysis. In particular, when it came to exploring who Yogi Bhajan was and the ideas he truly believed in.

The foundation for the 3HO Sikhs is Bhajan's claims that he received secret Sikh Yogic knowledge from a Tibetan Lama named Lilan Po, whose whereabouts only Bhajan knew. The knowledge given to Bhajan was supposedly knowledge imparted to Guru Nanak Ji's son, Sri Chand, by Nanak. According to the story, for 450 years the knowledge remained dormant until Yogi Bhajan came along and gave it a voice. The Tibetan Lama proclaimed that the knowledge was not for the Indians, including the Guru's Sikhs, but only for the Americans.[102]

Hmm, I think it's time to raise a red flag. The secret was only for the Americans? Wait a minute. The Guru was universal in his teachings and taught all the secrets he knew. The Guru was not in the business of excluding valuable knowledge from those who followed him.

Now, why only the Americans? First, the story Yogi Bhajan presents isn't within any ancient Sikh literature, and the story doesn't align with Sikhie history. The story is a construct of Bhajan's and the interests he represented.

Bhajan proclaimed that the secret he held was only for the Americans because the Americans would easily buy that idea. There are segments of the American population who already think they're deserving of ideas that no others hold.

The 3HO believe in ideas that the Sikh community doesn't believe in, and it's difficult to blame them. They were conned by a conman. Yogi Bhajan was a slithery character, and he understood how to sell a story. For that reason, without consulting any Sikh institution, Bhajan proclaimed himself the mini-Pope of the Sikhs in the Western Hemisphere. *"High Priest Guruchuran Singh Tohra...says that...Sikhs do not create such offices."*[103]

Such titles, which create another seat of power and bestow the privilege of initiating members into Guru Gobind Singh Ji's Khalsa, were never bestowed upon any Sikh, especially one who wasn't Khalsa or without great saintly merit. For him to proclaim himself as such is heretical.[104] Regardless, Bhajan gave himself extravagant titles he wasn't deserving of and he did that to add a sense of grandeur to his name and his movement.

It's apparent that Bhajan attempted to monopolize the Sikh faith in the West, and his ambitions didn't stop there. He also attempted to bring Christianity into his fold by making the claim that he was Jesus Christ. Along that line, he compared his humiliations and scandals to the suffering of Jesus.[105] That includes all the sex scandals he was involved in, for which the plaintiffs received millions by Bhajan's organization, the 3HO.

> *"Premka Khalsa alleged that Yogi Bhajan repeatedly physically and sexually assaulted her from November 1968 to November 1984...In court papers, she alleged that the yogi was sexually involved with various female followers, and that he ordered her to coordinate his sexual liaisons, including orgies, with other secretaries, which she refused to do".* She continues to state that *"the women in his inner circle were denied having a personal relationship with any other men".*[106]

> *"Colleen Hoskins, who worked seven months at his New Mexico residence, reports that men are scarcely seen there. He is served, she says, by a coterie of as many as 14 women, some of whom attend his baths, give him group massages, and take turns spending the night in his room while his wife sleeps elsewhere."*[107]

Another example of the several lawsuits pursued against Bhajan was that by Katherine Felt. She received an undisclosed amount to keep quiet.

Yogi Bhajan, with his apparent flaws, not only claimed he was Jesus but he also claimed that he was greater than the Sikh Guru was. Something no other Sikh saint in history has ever done. They all attributed their knowledge to the source they gained their knowledge from, *Sri Guru Granth Sahib Ji*.

The author, Dr. Trilochan Singh, writes:

> *"Wherever I went in the U.S.A. even people very friendly to Yogi Bhajan informed me that he pretended to have done more than Guru Gobind Singh did, and his vanity and ego maniac haughtiness had gone to the extent of saying in a gathering that he can even shake the gaddi (throne) of Guru Nanak. I did not take these stories seriously and refused to believe them. But I was shocked to read the afore-mentioned statements published within the last 12 months or so. When I saw these insulting remarks heaped on Guru Gobind Singh in print, the shock became unbearable."*

Yogi Bhajan also proclaimed that Guru Gobind was wrong when he instituted the Khalsa, he (Bhajan) has done more than Guru Gobind Singh could ever do, and he (Bhajan) was trying to correct Guru Gobind Singh Ji's mistakes.

If you know the history of the Great Gobind, you would know that very few men in history were able to accomplish what he did. Examining Bhajan's life, his accomplishments were far from touching the achievements of Guru Gobind Singh.

Lost to the illusions of empire, Bhajan also believed he was more divine than Guru Nanak was. Bhajan claimed he was able to shake Guru Nanak's very essence. But he stole his ideas and practices from the teachings of the Guru and then mixed in elements of Hinduism to make the claim that he knew more than the Sikh Guru.[108]

To reinforce his belief in his superiority, Bhajan has paintings of himself holding the Universe in his hands, as if he was the Master of all. The picture I'm referring to is on the following website: *http://gurmukhyoga.com/forum/index.php?id=392*. (You'll have to scroll down to see it).

163

Now, Yogi Bhajan, through his propaganda and misinformation, effectively pacified the Khalsa by misrepresenting the Khalsa to those who learnt about Sikhie from him. The Khalsa is an armed union of saint-soldiers, and each Singh or Kaur (a member of the Khalsa) personifies the idea of **Miri Piri**.

Instituted in 1699, the Khalsa's objectives are to uproot wickedness, protect the holy of all religion, protect Sikhie, and to defend against tyranny. The original members of the Khalsa, up until post-British rule, met the purposes of the Khalsa. By the time the British were done using the Khalsa for their own agenda, the Khalsa was a mere fraction of what it began as. Attempts are made to restore the Khalsa but outside interference continues to thwart most efforts. In the latest attempt to restore the Khalsa, during the late 70s to the late 90s, the Indian Government responded by attacking its own people and killing 250 000 Sikhs. *(Appendix A for more information).*

Having discussed the murder of 250 000 Sikhs with members of 3HO, it became clear that they held a biased viewpoint. They believe the Sikhs in Punjab were in the wrong and the Indian Government was justified in their attempt at wiping clear Sikhie thought. However, the overwhelming evidence suggests that the Indian Government was the villain and the Sikhs were protecting the Sikh way of life.

Evidence suggests that the Indian Government attempted to commit genocide and certain governments of the world, such as Australia, have respected that point of view. What 3HO members believe is the propaganda (political-spin) the Indian Government popularized. It was propaganda taught to 3HO members through Bhajan and the vast 3HO network. Again, adding credibility to the suggestion that groups like the Indian Intelligence Agency and the R.S.S. are influencing the beliefs of 3HO Sikhs.

3HO followers adhere to the appearance of Guru Gobind Singh Ji's Khalsa but not the objectives, and they can't seem to recognize tyranny. Nor have I ever heard of a 3HO Sikh sacrificing all to stand toe-to-toe with the wicked-doers as the Khalsa did and still attempts to do. The 3HO Sikhs are in appearance and not in substance. It would appear as if they adopted the look of the Khalsa but not the spirit. But that's Bhajan's doing and the innocent people who learnt from him and his organization aren't to blame.

Interestingly enough, the master of the Universe, Yogi Bhajan, who was the great corrector of mistakes, made the mistake of attempting to predict the future. Officially thrusting a dagger threw his claim of spiritual supremacy. During a 3HO Teachers meeting in Santa Cruz, New Mexico, in the year 1974, he predicted that in a decade dead bodies would be lying on the roads, tremendous sickness and insanity would overcome the nation (America), children would be orphans and people would eat them alive, and people would be jumping out of hospital windows.[109]

The West was contaminated by inaccurate Sikh practices and the beliefs taught by Yogi Bhajan and his followers. But the contemporary 3HO members refuse to believe they were misled. They would rather believe Yogi Bhajan was some sort of Messiah sent to the West to save them and correct the mistakes of the Sikh Guru, and even Jesus. An international campaign led by Gursant Singh, the son of a US Marine Corps Officer, to stop the misrepresentations by Yogi Bhajan Sikhs, is currently underway.[110]

Not surprisingly, 3HO is a business worth billions of dollars, and this wealth was partially accumulated because the organization doesn't pay their workers. If they do, it's very little. However, the profits do fatten the pockets of the leading 3HO members. Yogi Bhajan lived a very lavish lifestyle.

> *"The head of Yogi Bhajan's administration, and an editor and writer for his publications, Premka Khalsa said she worked an average of ten hours a day, five days a week and was paid $375 a month –and only that in her last three years with the group."*[111]

Furthermore, there are several lawsuits stating that Bhajan conned people into buying various items, property, and healing remedies.[112] He even tricked his followers into sending their children to schools in India, where his son-in-law profited from the manipulation.[113] Members of Bhajan's organization were also linked to criminal activities, as suggested by an investigator for the Monterey County District Attorney's Office. One member pleaded guilty to a scam that conned senior citizens for hundreds of thousands of dollars.[114]

Religious denominations come into existence for three principle reason, and in this case, 3HO was created to fulfill a personal agenda and to corrupt the beliefs of the root religion from which it attempts to stem from.

Black Sunshine

Opportune for religion, but tragic for the woman and man, the person is born unaware of the truth. Moreover, the human is born innocent and will trust almost all information presented as honest. As such, it's nearly impossible to know what isn't shown without digging through all the political rhetoric, the selfish insertions, and the out and out false information presented as honest.

Gods, Goddesses, and Rituals

Why does the institution of Hinduism have so many gods, goddesses, and rituals?

The contemporary Hindu faith believes in hundreds of thousands of gods and goddesses, and to compliment, hundreds of thousands of rituals. However, if you look at the *Vedas*, the oldest spiritual literature in the world--dating back to over 12 000 years, and the literature Hinduism stems from, there is only One Supreme Lord and Master of all the known and unknown.

There is only One Master but Hinduism accommodates countless gods, goddesses, and rituals, and they appear to create a wall, a wall between The Great Architect and the person. Instead of focusing on The Eternal, people pay homage to rituals, gods, and goddesses.

The prevailing theory amongst the academics is that the Brahmins, the high caste Hindu, introduced their own ideas into Hinduism to increase their power and influence--corrupting the *Vedas*. When reading the *Vedas*, I couldn't help but feel that idea resonate.

As claimed by holy men like Buddha, the true *Vedas*, declared by the Sage Kashyap, were celestially inspired. But with time, they were corrupted. With time, the *Vedas* grew to accommodate hundreds of thousands of gods, goddesses, and rituals.

When one of the highest caste Hindus wanted more wealth, power, and influence, he would create a god or goddess and a ritual to attract the people. The rituals, gods, or goddesses were meaningless, but something new always attracts attention.

That said, before the Brahmin would initiate any ritual, a monetary contribution from the seeker was expected. This expectation is now a part of the Hindu popular culture and collective intelligence. False holy people fleece the believer and line their own pockets.

Unfortunately, there isn't enough time to examine all the Hindu goddesses and gods; there are just too many. But I did make an interesting discovery after examining several of them. Some of the now gods or goddesses were once

169

actual people. These people were superhuman and able to access the third eye and the fourth dimension. More important, they were with an abnormally strong spiritual link to The Great Architect.

Some of the now gods and goddesses were people who understood the laws of the human condition and the laws of the absolute Universe. For that reason, during their physical existence, they were able to perform superhuman actions. For example, they could remote view, heal people, and foresee the future. In most cases, their superhuman qualities and achievements were what led the Brahmins to transform them into a demi-god or a demi-goddess. The Brahmins discarded their mortality and exploited only their miracle making powers. The congregation, blinded by the magic, were fooled by the propaganda.

Hinduism still practices the art of mislabelling men and women who have access to their third eye, access to The Primal Energy, and access to the ability to perform what most people would consider miracles as gods or goddesses. For example, they readily attempt to incorporate the Sikh Gurus into their system of gods and goddesses, even though the Gurus never considered the self a god.

Hinduism accommodates hundreds of thousands of gods, goddesses, and rituals, and alongside the explanations already given, some of the gods, goddesses, and rituals were not created for personal gain but to explain complex physical and metaphysical universal principles found within the ancient *Vedas*. A visual representation such as a goddess and ritual were useful tools to communicate and teach ideas.

Hinduism is a very convoluted religion, and like all the others, you'll find truths and you'll also discover fabrications. But a certain happening is unique to Hinduism, a certain happening that contributed to Hinduism housing so many gods, goddesses, and rituals.

Hinduism has a nasty habit of engulfing other religions in an attempt to Hinduize that religion. In the process of such an ugly practice, they typically end up adopting the saints and the practices of that engulfed religion. After adding their own twist, they usually transform the saints into gods or goddesses.

An excellent example of a doctrine penetrated and marginalized by Hinduism is Buddha's teachings. Although Buddha is of Indian origin and Buddha's teachings first took root there, his teachings were slowly corrupted by Hinduism and marginalized.

Buddhism was unable to grow and flourish in the place of its origin because of Hinduism, in particular, the high caste Hindus. Buddhist teachings challenge their power base, the caste system, and to sustain their power, Buddhism had to be eliminated, contaminated, or incorporated into the Hindu faith. Buddha is a good example of the many superhuman individuals who Hinduism transformed into a Hindu god.

Buddha's teachings survived and they were able to take root in Tibet over 1000 years after Buddha's ascendance. Padmasambhava of Hindustan (India) introduced Buddhism to Tibet, and the type of Buddhism he introduced is the most popular type in the world. However, after examining Tibetan Buddhist thought and practice, one can't help but notice certain Hindu ideas within it.

For example:

1) Tibetans who follow Buddhism hang paper or a piece of cloth on a string with their troubles or their wishes of prosperity written on them. However, Buddha never recommended practices such as that. Buddha focused on the use of the consciousness to alleviate troubles or to prosper. However, Hinduism readily practices such things.

2) A symbol first used by Hinduism, and readily found in Buddhism, is the "Dharma Chakra".

3) Buddha in often illustrated with a mark on his head, a mark similar to the Hindu "tilak"--a mark that Hindus use to represent the "third eye". The depiction is another plausible representation of the merger.

4) Although the contemporary Buddhist is regularly seen with his or her head shaven, and contemporary depictions of Buddha show a shaven head, all the ancient depictions of Buddha show him with long hair. However, the high caste Hindu, the Brahmin Hindu, adorns a shaven head. It would seem that Hinduism removed the hair of Buddha to represent Buddha more like a Brahmin. Maybe, that's why the "tilak" was applied to the forehead of the

great Buddha, who believed more in the power of the conscious and subconscious than the illusion of the material such as the "tilak".

The institution of Hinduism readily attempts to absorb other religions. Buddhism is an excellent example of the happening. For such reasons, Hinduism accommodates countless celestial spirits. Unfortunately, the created gods, goddesses, and rituals have existed for so long that they're above debate and taken as fact by the contemporary Hindu faith.

In the end, there is good reason to believe in Brahma (the creator of the Universe), in Vishnu (the preserver of the Universe), and in Shiva (the destroyer of the Universe)--the three primary Hindu demi-gods. Their existence is plausible. But please remember the *Vedas* and The Creator that created all of the plausible demi-gods. Without The Ultimate Creator, there would be no Brahma, Vishnu, or Shiva, and even they bow before the Great Creator. Tell me--who is more worthy of praise, the created or that which created?

Misdirection

Rituals mostly misdirect the flock, and the true causes of a mystical phenomenon are typically sounds, vibrations, intentions, etc.

Religious leaders misdirect the audience with fancy rituals so to keep the common person ignorant, thus, retaining their power and position. Knowledge can sometimes empower a person, and simultaneously, take power away from those who hold it.

Hinduism and Feeding Statues

Wasting food does not demonstrate a belief in God, especially when your neighbour is starving. But Hinduism readily encourages the wasting of food so to appease one demi-god or another.

I've seen litres of milk poured over a rock and litres left behind, plates of prepared food given to a statue, and bundles of wheat and rice gifted to an inanimate object--all in the hope to gain favour from a particular spirit.

The idea of wasting food to satisfy an entity that doesn't eat makes no sense. The act makes even less sense when that food could be used to feed a hungry person. In the nation where Hinduism is dominant, India, the hungry are everywhere.

The idea of gifting food and other items such as clothing, another common offering, to a demi-god, is an idea created generations ago by the Brahmin Hindus, so they could benefit from the offering.

During one of my visits to an Indian Hindu place of worship, a place where people were specifically asked to bring, among other things, alcohol, lamb, and/or a chicken as an offering. The supposed holy people there drank and ate very well. The first thing I noticed was a so-called holy person, outside the gates to the temple, passed-out drunk. I also observed that most occupants of this supposed holy site were overweight--they ate well.

The supposed holy people at this particular site drank and ate like kings and queens, and their fraud isn't unique, countless other sites all over India are home to con artists who do the same. I guess some people will believe anything a so-called holy person suggests, and other people are afraid to question a supposed mediator to the spiritual realm, regardless if their suggestions are foolish and illogical. Why else would innocent people attempt to feed statues?

Offerings are not unique to Hinduism. Judaism too practices the same type of behaviour.

> *"If his offering be a burnt sacrifice of the herd, let him offer a male without blemish: he shall offer it of his own voluntary will at*

the door of the tabernacle of the congregation before the LORD."--(Leviticus 1:3)

"And he shall bring his trespass offering unto the LORD for his sin which he hath sinned, a female from the flock, a lamb or a kid of the goats, for a sin offering; and the priest shall make an atonement for him concerning his sin."--(Leviticus 5:6)

Offerings, and other peculiarities such as ritual sacrifices, were acceptable forms of worship in a particular age in the cycle of the four epochs. But the era humanity is currently in, the **Age of Iron**, isn't conducive to those types of practices. In this era, God's Name is the only salvation.

The Ungodly Caste System

It might come as a surprise to some and Gandhi endorsed the inhumane Caste System in India. He also worked to bring other religions under the Hindu philosophy.

The Hindu Caste System is a hierarchy of inherited occupational duties and social status. It divides the Hindu people, from birth, into various occupations and the social status that accompanies it. It doesn't matter if a person is talented otherwise, and until death, a person is stuck in the category they were born into.

The four principle castes, presented highest to lowest, are: 1) The priestly (Brahmins). 2) The warriors (Kshatriyas). 3) The Merchants (Vaishyas). 4) And the untouchables (Shudras). As you can probably guess, most are Shudras.

The idea of the Hindu Caste System is centered on the universal principle of Karma. The caste into which an individual is born, is the result of their Karma. For that reason, one must remain within that caste until death. However, the universal principle of Karma doesn't operate under such an inhumane cloud. Even the ancient Vedic literature, from which Hinduism stems from, doesn't claim what the Hindu Caste System suggests.

Karma does play a part in an individual's birth, life, and death, but an individual isn't trapped to their Karma. An individual's Karma can be improved, remain neutral, or take a downward turn. The people at the bottom of the Caste System were misinformed, and they were taught to believe that an individual's Karma is unchangeable.

Sadly, because of the propaganda conditioned as a collective truth, the untouchables are enslaved to the most unclean, polluted, diseased, and unhygienic occupations. No matter if the person had the mind of Einstein, or the strength of the biblical Samson, or the spirit of Mujaddid Alif Sani. If born an untouchable, an untouchable an individual must remain.

The untouchables were forbidden, and still are, from such things as entering temples, living amongst the villagers, and drinking from the wells the higher castes drink from. Some Brahmins even take offence if the shadow of an untouchable falls upon one of their caste.

> *"In the dwelling of the womb, there is no ancestry or social status.*
> *All have originated from the Seed of God. Tell me, O Pandit, O*
> *religious scholar: since when have you been a Brahmin? Don't*
> *waste your life by continually claiming to be a Brahmin. If you*
> *are indeed a Brahmin, born of a Brahmin mother, then why didn't*
> *you come by some other way? How is that you are a Brahmin,*
> *and I am of a low social status? How is it that I am formed of*
> *blood, and you are made of milk? Says Kabeer, one who*
> *contemplates God is said to be a Brahmin among us. || 4 || 7 ||"*--
> (Sri Guru Granth Sahib Ji, ang 324 of 1430)

It would seem that politics led to the introduction of the Caste System, and those of higher status used and still use the Caste System to ensure their elite status. Unchallenged, the Caste System is a means for families with good occupations and status to preserve that occupation and status for generations to come. And because of the engrained Karmatic beliefs, the lowest caste isn't likely to challenge the establishment of the Caste System and those who benefit from it.

The Indian Government readily stands on the international stage and claims that the Caste System isn't an issue. But the reality on the ground is much different from the propaganda the government is attempting to sell. From the very beginning, as demonstrated by the much-overrated Gandhi, the Caste System wasn't on the list of things to remove or improve.

The argument is made that those who shared Gandhi's belief were working to free India from British Imperialism only to enslave the Indian people to the Caste System and the Indian Elite. Don't be fooled, the people of India are still governed by interests that have no interest in them. The only difference between colonial rule and the current rule is the skin colour of those who rule. Today, Indians yoke Indians.

The reason most are unaware of Gandhi's dark-side, such as his belief in the Caste System, is because that's what the British wanted. The British depicted Gandhi as a pious individual who passively freed India, so to keep the other British slaves violence free. However, Gandhi's passivism didn't free India.

177

Individuals such as Bhagat Singh did and their use of violence was instrumental in defeating the British.

You see, defeated with ease is a group of Gandhis; conquered with ease is a passive uprising. Costly are those with AKs and machetes. An empire could be shattered to pieces. For that reason, the British promoted Gandhi as the individual who secured Indian independence.

After the World Wars, the British were financially broke and their military was near death. For those reasons, they were unable to maintain control over their colonies when those colonies acted violently to gain their freedom. After Indian independence, the British were afraid the happenings in India would inspire their other colonies. Before those colonies could discover how the Indians gained their freedom, the British began a propaganda campaign that popularized the peaceful Gandhi as the liberator. The British were hoping that their other colonies would mimic Gandhi's passive movement and not that of Bhagat Singh. Unarmed resistance is so much easier and cheaper to eliminate.

Chapter One Endnotes

1. Thomas S. Asbridge, The First Crusade: A New History (Oxford University Press: New York, 2004), p. 1-3. / H.E.J. Cowdrey. "Pope Urban II's Preaching of the First Crusade." The Crusades; the essential readings. Ed. by Thomas F. Madden. (Blackwell Publishing: Oxford, UK; Malden, Ma, 2002). / Jonathan Riley-Smith. "Crusading as an Act of Love." The Crusades; the essential readings. Ed. by Thomas F. Madden. (Blackwell Publishing: Oxford, UK; Malden, Ma, 2002).

2. John France, The Crusaders and the Expansion of Catholic Christendom, 1000-1714 (New York: Routledge, 2005). / Jonathan Riley-Smith, The Crusades: a history; second edition (Yale University Press: New Haven, 2005).

3. "Indian Residential Schools Settlement Agreement: May 8th, 2006." Indian Residential Schools Settlement – Official Court Website. [http://www.residentialschoolsettlement.ca/Settlement.pdf], January, 2009. / Art Gallery of Windsor, New World – old world: eurocentric perceptions of first nations people and the landscape (Windsor: Art Gallery of Windsor, 1997). / Tim Giago, Children Left Behind: dark legacy of Indian mission boarding schools (Clear Light Pub.: Santa Fe, N.M., 2006).

4. Joseph Perez, The Spanish Inquisition: a history (Profile: London, 2004).

5. James M. Blaut, The Colonizer's Model of the World: geographical diffusionism and Eurocentric history (Guildford Press: New York, 1993).

6. Jack Nelson-Pallmeyer, Is Religion Killing Us?: violence in the Bible and the Quran (Continuum International Publishing Group: New York, 2005), p. 33.

7. Jerrold M. Post, Leaders and their Followers in a Dangerous World: the psychology of political behaviour (Cornell University Press: New York, 2004), p. 139.

8. Charles Selengut, Sacred Fury: understanding religious violence (Rowman Altamira: California, 2003), p. 226.

9. Robert Spencer, The Politically Incorrect Guide to Islam and the Crusades (Regnery Publishing: America, 2005), p. 54.

10. Ibid., p. 107 – 120.

11. Patrick Brantlinger, Rule of Darkness: British literature and imperialism, 1830-1914 (Cornell University Press: Ithaca, N.Y., 1988). / Homi Bhabha, The Location of Culture (Routledge: London; New York, 2004). / Robert Giddings, ed. Literature and Imperialism (Macmillan: Houndmills, 1991).

12. David Criswell, The Rise and Fall of the Holy Roman Empire: from Charlemagne to Napoleon (Publish America: Maryland, 2005). / Desmond O'Grady, Beyond the Empire: Rome and the church from Constantine to Charlemagne (Crossroad Publishing: New York, 2001). / Nino Lo Bello, The Vatican Empire (Trident Press: New York, 1969).

13. Richard Heber Newton, The Right and Wrong Uses of the Bible (John W. Lovell, 1883), p. 50. [http://www.google.com/books?id=bww-AAAAYAAJ&dq=The+Right+and+Wrong+Uses+of+the+Bible]

14. Ernan McMullin, ed. The Church and Galileo (University of Notre Dame Press: Indiana, 2005).

15. (Kent C. Condie and Robert E. Sloan, Origin and Evolution of Earth: principles of historical geology (Prentice Hall: NJ, 1998).

16. Robert Spencer, Religion of Peace?: why Christianity is and Islam isn't (Regnery Publishing: Washington, 2007), p. 111.

17. David Daniels and Jack T. Chick, Did the Catholic Church Give use the Bible? (Chick Publications: California: 2005) p. 57-59.

18. Kersten Holger, Jesus Lived in India: his unknown life before and after the crucifixion (Penguin Books: India, 2001) / Nicolas B. Notovitch, The Unknown Life of Jesus Christ (Nababharat: Calcutta, 1981) / Levi H. Dowling, The Aquarian Gospel of Jesus the Christ (Biblio Publishing, 2009) p. 83-137.

19. P.A.H. Seymour, The Birth of Christ: Exploding the Myth (Virgin Publishing: London, 1999). / Michael R. Monlar, The Star of Bethlehem: The Legacy of the Magi (Rutgers University Press: NJ, 1999). / Stephen Vidano, Director, The Star of Bethlehem, 2007.

20. John Cornwell, Hitler's Pope: the secret history of Pius XII (Viking: New York, 1999). / Gordon Charles Zahn, German Catholics and Hitler's War: a study in social control (Sheed and Ward: New York, 1962).

21. Jacques LeGoff, The Birth of Purgatory (University of Chicago Press: Chicago, 1981). / Loraine Boettner, Roman Catholicism – Chapter Ten: Purgatory (P & R Publishing: NJ, 1989)

22. Loraine Boettner, Roman Catholicism – Chapter Nine: The Confessional (P & R Publishing: NJ, 1989)

23. Jacques LeGoff, The Birth of Purgatory (University of Chicago Press: Chicago, 1981) p. 52.

24. John Henry Hopkins, The History of the Confessional (Harper: London, 1850) p. 11
[http://books.google.ca/books?id=hMIHAAAAQAAJ&pg=PR6&dq=The+Confessional+and+false]

25. S. Acharya, Suns of God: Krishna, Buddha and Christ Unveiled (Adventures Unlimited Press: Illinois, 2004) p.205-206. / The Vishnu Purana. Trans. by Horace Hayman Wilson: 1840. / Larry Charles, Director, Religulous, 2008.

26. Unknown, The Bible and the People (1853), p. 60.
[http://www.google.com/books?id=tjMEAAAQAAJ&dq=The+Bible+and+the+People]

27. Joseph Priestly, An History of the Corruption of Christianity (University of Lausanne, 1782), p.80-283.
[http://www.google.com/books?id=y6AUAAAAQAAJ&printsec=frontcover&dq=An+History+of+the+Corruption+of+Christianity]

28. Garry Wills, Papal Sin: structures of deceit (Image Books/Doubleday: New York, 2001)./ Brandon Toropov, The Complete Idiot's Guide to the Popes and the Papacy (Alpha Books: America, 2001), p. 47-56.

29. Edward W. Said, Culture and Imperialism (Random House: New York, 1993)

30. Ann Graham Brock, <u>Mary Magdalene, The First Apostle: The Struggle for Authority</u> (Harvard University Press: Massachusetts, 2002). / Meere Lester, <u>The Everything Mary Magdalene Book: The life and legacy of Jesus's most misunderstood disciple</u> (Adams Media: Cincinnati, OH, 2006). / Jean Leloup, <u>Gospel of Mary Magdalene</u> (Inner tradition: Vermont, 2002).

31. Adrian Thatcher, <u>The Savage Text: the use and abuse of the Bible</u> (Wiley-Blackwell: Malden, MA, 2008), p. 39-49.

32. Eugen J. Weber, <u>Apocalypses: prophecies, cults and millennial beliefs through the ages</u> (Random House of Canada: Toronto, 1999).

33. Ibid.

34. Alexander George and Jerrold M. Post, <u>Leaders and their Followers in a Dangerous World: the psychology of political behaviour</u> (Cornell University Press: New York, 2004), p. 135-136.

35. Charles Selengut, <u>Sacred Fury: understanding religious violence</u> (Rowman Altamira: California, 2003), p. 101.

36. Alexander George and Jerrold M. Post,<u> Leaders and their Followers in a Dangerous World: the psychology of political behaviour</u> (Cornell University Press: New York, 2004), p. 141.

37. Gershom Gorenberg,<u> The End of Days: fundamentalism and the struggle for the Temple Mount </u>(Free Press: New York, 2000). / Adrian Thatcher, <u>The Savage Text: the use and abuse of the Bible </u>(Wiley-Blackwell: United Kingdom, 2008), p. 57 -63. / Victoria Clark, <u>Allies for Armageddon: the rise of Christian Zionism</u> (Yale University Press: New Haven; London, 2007).

38. Charles Selengut, <u>Sacred Fury: understanding religious violence</u> (Rowman Altamira: California, 2003), p. 103.

39. Adrian Thatcher, <u>The Savage Text: the use and abuse of the Bible</u> (Wiley-Blackwell: United Kingdom, 2008), p. 57.

40. James Penton, <u>Apocalypse Delayed: the story of Jehovah's Witnesses</u> (University of Toronto Press Incorporated: Toronto, 1985), p. 18.

41. Ibid., p. 22.

42. Ibid., p. 44.

43. Jerry L. Walls, The Oxford Handbook of Eschatology (Oxford University Press: New York, 2007), p. 196.

44. Ibid., p. 196-197.

45. Bart D. Ehrman, Whose Words Is it? The story behind who changed the New Testament and Why (Continuum International Publishing Group LTD: New York, 2008), p. 10.

46. Translated by George Eliot, The Life of Jesus: critically examined (C. Blanchard, 1860), p. 41-54.

47. John S. Vaughan, Concerning the Holy Bible: Its use and abuse (Benziger Bros: New York, 1904), p. 11-12.

48. Peter Stravinskas, The Catholic Church and the Bible (Ignatius Press: San Francisco, 1996), p. 17.

49. Bart D. Ehrman, The Orthodox Corruption of Scripture: the effect of early Christological controversies in the text of the New Testament (Oxford University Press: USA, 1996), p. xi.

50. Mark D. Roberts, Can We Trust the Gospels? investigating the reliability of Mathew, Mark, Luke, and John (Good News Publishers: Illinois, 2007), p. 27.

51. John S. Vaughan, Concerning the Holy Bible: Its use and abuse (Benziger Bros: New York, 1904), p. 12.

52. DC Parker and Jeff Childers, Transmission and Reception: New Testament text-critical and exegetical studies (Gorgias Press: New Jersey, 2006), p. 40.

53. Mark D. Roberts, Can We Trust the Gospels?: investigating the reliability of Mathew, Mark, Luke, and John (Good News Publishers: Illinois, 2007), p. 28.

54. John S. Vaughan, <u>Concerning the Holy Bible: Its use and abuse</u> (Benziger Bros: New York, 1904), p. 14.

55. Bart D. Ehrman, <u>Misquoting Jesus; the story behind who changed the Bible and why</u> (Harper San Francisco: San Francisco, 2007), p. 5.

56. Bart D. Ehrman, <u>Whose Words Is it? The story behind who changed the New Testament and Why</u> (Harper San Francisco: San Francisco, 2005), p.7.

57. Ibid.

58. Bart D. Ehrman, <u>Lost Scriptures: books that did not make it into the New Testament</u> (Oxford University Press: Oxford; New York, 2003).

59. Christians Timothy David Barnes, <u>Constantine and Eusebius</u> (Harvard University Press: Massachusetts, 1981), p. 216.

60. David L. Dungan, <u>Constantine's Bible: politics and the making of the New Testament</u> (Fortress Press: Philadelphia, 2006), pg 112.

61. Bart D. Ehrman, <u>Truth and Fiction in the Da Vinci Code: a historian reveals what we really know about Jesus, Mary Magdalene, and Constantine</u> (Oxford University: New York, 2004), p. 98.

62. Alexander Campbell and John Baptist Purcell, <u>A Debate on the Roman Catholic Religion: held in Sycamore Street Meeting House</u>, Cincinnati, from the 13th to the 21st of January, 1837 (J.A. James, 1837), p. 55.

63. Max Arthur Macauliffe, <u>The Sikh Religion, Volume 1</u> (Forgotten Books, 2008), p. 60.
[http://www.google.com/books?id=E0UwOOjrjGAC&dq=The+Sikh+Religion]

64. David L. Dungan, <u>Constantine's Bible: politics and the making of the New Testament</u> (Fortress Press: Philadelphia, 2006), p. 112.

65. Ibid., p. 109.

66. Ibid., p. 116.

67. William Anderson Scott, The Bible and Politic: or, An humble plea for equal, perfect, absolute religious freedom, and against all sectarianism in our public schools (H.H. Bancroft, 1859), p. 83.

68. David L. Dungan, Constantine's Bible: politics and the making of the New Testament (Fortress Press: Philadelphia, 2006), p. 102.

69. Ibid., p. 96.

70. Ibid., p. 125.

71. Adrian Thatcher, The Savage Text: the use and abuse of the Bible (Wiley-Blackwell: United Kingdom, 2008), p. 3-4.

72. Alexander Campbell and John Baptist Purcell, A Debate on the Roman Catholic Religion: held in Sycamore Street Meeting House, Cincinnati, from the 13th to the 21st of January, 1837 (J.A. James, 1837), p. 263.

73. John S. Vaughan, Concerning the Holy Bible: Its use and abuse (Benziger Bros: New York, 1904), p. 81.

74. Jack Nelson-Pallmeyer, Is Religion Killing Us?: violence in the Bible and the Quran (Continuum International Publishing Group: New York, 2005), p.32.

75. Ibid., p. 34-35.

76. Richard Heber Newton, The Right and Wrong Uses of the Bible (John W. Lovell, 1883), p. 43. [http://www.google.com/books?id=bww-AAAAYAAJ&dq=The+Right+and+Wrong+Uses+of+the+Bible]

77. Joseph Ennemoser, The History of Magic. Trans. By W. Howitt (1854), p. 132.
[http://www.google.com/books?id=dhoHAAAAQAAJ&dq=The+history+of+magic,+tr.+by+W.+Howitt.+To+which+is+added+an+appendix+of+the+most+remarkable+and+best+authenticated+stories+of+apparitions+%5B%26c.%5D+selected+by+M.+Howitt]

78. John Barton and Julia Bowden, The Original Story: God, Israel, and the world (Wm. B. Eerdmans Publishing: Michigan, 2005), p. 262. / S.A.

Nigosian, The Zoroastrian Faith: tradition and modern research (McGill-Queen's University Press: Montreal, 1993) p. 71-97.

79. Alexander Heidel, The Gilgamesh Epic and Old Testament Parallels (University of Chicago: Chicago, 1949).

80. (editor and translator) Stephanie Dalley, Myths from Mesopotamia: creation, the flood, Gilgamesh, and others (Oxford University Press: New York, 1998).

81. Remi Brague, The Law of God: the philosophical history of an idea. Trans. by Lydia G. Cochrane (University of Chicago Press: United States, 2007), p. 70-71.

82. Ibid., p. 71.

83. Dave MacPherson, The Rapture Plot (South Carolina: Millennium III Publishers, 2000). / David B. Currie, Rapture: The end-times error that leaves the bible behind (Sophia Institute Press: Manchester, NH, 2004).

84. Wilson H. Speed, Rapture: A Dangerous Deception (Xulon Press: Longwood, Fl, 2009) p. 113.

85. Ibid., p. 115.

86. Alice K. Turner, The History of Hell (Harcourt Brace & Company: New York, 1993). / "What the hell is Hell?" Tentmaker Ministries [http://www.what-the-hell-is-hell.com], January, 2009.

87. Thomas Thayer, The Origins and History of the Doctrine of Endless Punishment (Kessinger Publishing: Montana, 2007) p. 74-97.

88. Ibid., p. 81-82.

89. Matthias Bejer, A Violent God-image: an introduction to the work of Eugen Drewermann (Continuum: New York, 2004).

90. Cambridge Master of Arts, The Bible history of Satan. Is he a fallen angel? (1858).

[http://www.google.com/books?id=EqkCAAAAQAAJ&dq=The+Bible+histor
y+of+Satan.+Is+he+a+fallen+angel%3F+By+a+Cambridge+master+of+arts]

91. Bart D. Ehrman, Misquoting Jesus; the story behind who changed the Bible
and why (San Francisco: Harper San Francisco, 2007).

92. The 3HO and how they differ from Real Sikhism. Video uploaded February
13, 2012. [www.youtube.com/watch?v=0eDRbehhDZA], accessed March 1,
2013.

93. Charles Y. Glock, The New Religious Consciousness (California:
University of California Press, 1976), p. 14. / The Gurmukh Yoga Forum
[http://gurmukhyoga.com/forum/index.php?id=392], March1, 2013.

94. 3HO Kundalini Yoga [http://www.3ho.org/march-2013-numerology],
March 1, 2013.

95. Charles Y. Glock, The New Religious Consciousness (California:
University of California Press, 1976), p. 19.

96. Joseph T. O'Connell, Milton Israel and Willard Gurdon Oxtoby, Sikh
history and religion in the twentieth century (India: Manohar Publications,
1990), p. 346.

97. Guru Dharam, Khalsa and Darryl O'Keeffe, The Kundalini Yoga
Experience: Bringing Body, Mind and Spirit Together (New Your, NY: Gaia
Books Limited, 2002), p. 17.

98. Kim Douglas, High Desert: A Journey of Survival and Hope (Illinois:
Baha'i Publishing, 2009), p. 13.

99. The Gurmukh Yoga Forum
[http://www.gurmukhyoga.com/forum/index.php?mode=page&id=1], March 1,
2013.

100. Religio-Political Talk [http://religiopoliticaltalk.com/yogi-bhajan-in-the-
news-ex-members-talk-of-heartache-and-betrayal-years-later/], March 1, 2013.

101. The Sikh Archives [http://www.sikharchives.com/?p=9745], March 1,
2013.

102. Dr. Trilochan Singh, Sikhism and Tantric Yoga (Ludhiana, India: Dr. Trilochan Singh, 1977), p. 141.

103. Time Magazine, Yogi Bhajan's Synthetic Sikhism (September 5, 1977).

104. Dr. Trilochan Singh, Sikhism and Tantric Yoga (Ludhiana, India: Dr. Trilochan Singh, 1977), p. 121.

105. Dr. Trilochan Singh, Sikhism and Tantric Yoga (Ludhiana, India: Dr. Trilochan Singh, 1977), p. 113.

106. The Register-Guard [http://projects.registerguard.com/csp/cms/sites/web/news/cityregion/24671927-41/yogi-khalsa-bhajan-leaders-members.csp], March 1, 2013.

107. Rick A. Ross Institute [http://www.rickross.com/reference/3ho/3ho94.html], March 1, 2013.

108. Dr. Trilochan Singh, Sikhism and Tantric Yoga (Ludhiana, India: Dr. Trilochan Singh, 1977), p. 148.

109. Rick A. Ross Institute [http://www.rickross.com/reference/3ho/3ho13.html], March 1, 2013.

110. The Gurmukh Yoga Forum [http://www.gurmukhyoga.com], March 1, 2013.

111. The Register-Guard [http://projects.registerguard.com/csp/cms/sites/web/news/cityregion/24671927-41/yogi-khalsa-bhajan-leaders-members.csp], March 1, 2013.

112. Love to Know Yoga [http://yoga.lovetoknow.com/Yogi_Bhajan_Criticism], March 1, 2013.

113. Rick A. Ross Institute [http://www.rickross.com/reference/3ho/3ho47.html], March 1, 2013.

114. Religio-Political Talk [http://religiopoliticaltalk.com/yogi-bhajan-in-the-news-ex-members-talk-of-heartache-and-betrayal-years-later/], March 1, 2013.

Chapter 2
Angels and Demons

To function through the ugly half of the mind's duality doesn't really make long-term sense, and that because of God and death. But someone forgot to tell the people who built and build the manmade world.

Life

The end is the greatest equalizer of all--blind to wealth, religion, and colour. Man can choose to ignore his humanity but death will always remember.

If existence after death is a Universal absolute like all the holy people suggest, then it's the invisible within the human condition that will continue to exist. Why? Well, the body can't escape death but the soul has the potential to.

In accordance, the truest life purpose can only be to love the immortal within (The Light within). That is, if a person would like a good existence after the body perishes.

Just as the body and the mind must be developed to extract, gather, and store the material resources required to live well within a material world, the same might be true of the invisible. It's important to develop the invisible condition to acquire that good existence after the body falls, and the invisible can only be understood and loved through the beautiful half of the mind's dichotomy.

However, no person is above the laws of his or her surroundings. If the information isn't present, how can a person learn it and become it? The truth must first dominate a person's environments so a person can translate and love immortality.

To that end, it would appear that we have a long way to go before we can love the invisible. **The built world** disguises the natural, and it forgot to love the soul. Furthermore, the information it circulates isn't the information required to live and die truthful.

An attitude adjustment is required. **The machine** needs a virtuous consciousness to filter out the information that threatens spiritual development, and the mindset should be adjusted so the "I" can see its place within the body fortress. Perhaps then, together, we could ask with true purpose, what is our truest purpose?

But spiritual development is in direct contradiction with industrialism, the contemporary market, and the consumer culture. It's in conflict because it threatens profit. Perhaps, that's why the person is taught to give little attention to the realm of the spirit. If an individual valued spiritual progress more than the consumption of the material and the senses, the money-makers would make less money. Not only that, the general public would demand more from their leaders--more God oriented behaviour.

"The living, the departed, and the yet-to-be-born seek their great successes from Him. The souls of the righteous shall eternally be strong. The wrongful shall experience repeated failures. The Wise God has, through His sovereignty, established these principles."--(Gathas: 10-7)

Like a sesame seed squeezed for its oil, it's as if popular religion and popular culture are attempting to press the spirit from the corporeal.

The Duality in You and Me

Such things as kindness, compassion, empathy, and truth are compromised because the selfish is nurtured to dominate. I see the compromise in an everyday life and I'm sure you've also witnessed it.

All the popular religions would agree that the mind suffers from duality. It's a natural happening. The two types of cognitive conditions a person accommodates are the beautiful and the selfish. Each condition is constituted by different beliefs and different cognitive units (cognitive units eventually mediated by a person's value system).

The Beautiful Cognitive Condition
The beautiful cognitive condition, also known as "the collective cognitive condition" and "the angelic half", develops, houses, nurtures, and reinforces a value system constituted by such beliefs and wants as the following: contentment, compassion, truth, unconditional love, humility, virtue, righteousness, empathy, **self-actualization**, a transitive conscious condition, rationality, emotional stability, a desire for knowledge, the soul ("The Light Within"), a spiritual life purpose (a life purpose before and beyond a secular purpose), a sense of oneness with humanity, and a collective ego.

Collective ego
The ego represents the belief of the self, and although the substance of the ego is learned, the shell that houses that substance is innate. What's more, the ego is the captain of both cognitive conditions and a person will grow to develop either a dominant collective ego or a dominant selfish ego. The beliefs mentioned in the previous paragraph constitute the collective ego.

The Ugly Cognitive Condition
To describe the ugly half of the mind's dichotomy, the phrases "the selfish cognitive condition" and "the demonic half" are also used. The dominant characteristics of a selfish cognitive condition are those that:

1) Suppress, weaken, contradict, or disguise the elements of the angelic half.

2) Nurture only sensual fulfilment, a selfish existence, sensory satisfaction, individuality, and self-interest.

195

3) Separate the self from humanity, communities, other people, The Absolute, the spirit, the Universe, and the planet.

4) Detail the individual with a higher value than humanity, other people, communities, death, The Absolute, the spirit, the Universe, and the planet.

5) Develop and nurture the selfish ego, and the destructive elements that validate the existence of the selfish ego.

Selfish ego
The beliefs mentioned above constitute the selfish ego. In addition, the four destructive elements heavily influence the selfish ego. The four destructive elements within the mind are anger, lust, attachment, and greed. The destructive agents are so for several reasons. They intensify the alienation of the mind from the collective cognitive condition and the behaviour and thoughts it generates. They give rise for a person to hurt another. They build and reinforce thoughts that strengthen the domination of a selfish cognitive condition. And they have a nasty habit of destroying the person from within while alienating the mind from spiritual intention.

1) Anger is an innate emotional unit of the mind, and when it predominantly influences the mind, the mind turns onto the self. That state of perception naturally limits the information used by the mind's decision-making process.

2) Lust is an innate ability of the mind, and it represents an intense and irrational want. Under the inductions of lust, the mind morphs into an island and is unable to construct thoughts outside the information that comprises the irrational want.

3) Attachment is an innate ability of the mind, and the term represents a mind unable to let go of a particular external or internal stimulation (memory, belief, or want). An attachment results in the narrowing of a person's awareness, and detachment from the stimulant usually causes the mind and body extreme pain and suffering.

196

4) Greed is a constructed want, and it represents an irrational and unmastered appetite. The term is applicable to the senses as much as it is to an irrational appetite for material objects. Like the others, greed alienates the mind from the power of the collective cognitive condition and all that follows.

The agents of the selfish or the agents of the collective are doorways to the entire condition. When an element of a cognitive condition such as anger is dominantly influencing the place where thoughts are determined, that component will entice other elements of the selfish into a state of preparedness. Each aspect of a condition is linked to the other elements of that condition.

When either condition is dominant, the many other beliefs and wants an individual constructs will be framed by the foremost condition. Likewise, the other cognitive units with the potential to motivate motion, and the type of information an individual will seek, will be guided by the dominant condition.

Interestingly, the elements of each condition complement each other, and the elements of each cognitive condition contradict the elements of the other. It would seem that they naturally fall into two camps, and because of this happening, to neglect the agents of the collective is to nurture the selfish, and to neglect the elements of the demonic is to nurture the angelic.

For the most part, a person volleys between the two conditions. However, a person will naturally grow to dominantly function through one of the two conditions, the half most strengthened and stimulated.

For economic reasons, the condition most strengthened and stimulated by the contemporary world is the selfish.

The two types of cognitive conditions a person accommodates are the beautiful and the ugly, and all the popular religions would agree that of the two, the first has greater importance. The selfish condition produces a state of being that isn't aligned to the heavens--the resonance it produces denies a celestial experience and pollutes a person's aura (magnetic field). The aura a person is under influences the experiences a person will attract. Negative thoughts and feelings only bring about negative experiences. All thoughts have invisible consequences, as demonstrated by Emoto's *Water Experiment*, and the experiment shows that the thoughts and feelings produced by the beautiful do not produce a chaotic presence, but the thoughts and feelings generated by the ugly half of the mind do. A chaotic presence denies spiritual progression and erects a barrier between the person and God's Spirit. Without God's Spirit, the Word will not be experienced, and without the Word, liberation is unattainable.

If you're familiar with sacred-geometry, you'll appreciate that the shapes produced by thoughts filtered through the beautiful half of the mind also create specific, beautiful, and meaningful shapes. The second volume discusses sacred-geometry.

Additionally, the selfish condition restricts a person's ability to meditate and it has a habit of harassing the place of thought when an individual is attempting to silence the mind. The beautiful condition doesn't have the same distracting effect.

The beautiful is the better of the two and it cocoons the ideal state of mind--an awareness conducive to spiritual progress. But unfortunately, our collective intelligence and our popular culture purposely strive to nurture the other half.

"Knowing others is wisdom, knowing yourself is Enlightenment."--Lao Tzu

"Now, the two foremost mentalities, known to be imaginary twins, are the better and the bad in thoughts, words, and deeds. Of these the beneficent choose correctly, but not so the maleficent.

Now, when the two mentalities first got together, they created "life" and "not-living." Until the end of existence, the worst mind shall be for the wrongful, and the best mind shall be for the righteous.

Of these two mentalities, the wrongful mentality chose worst actions, and the most progressive mentality, as steadfast as rock, chose righteousness. Therefore, those who would please the Wise God, may do so by choosing true actions.

Between these two, the seekers of false gods did not decide correctly, because delusion came to them in their deliberations. Therefore, they chose the worst mind, rushed in wrath, and afflicted the human existence.

But to the person who chooses correctly, comes endurance of body and steadfast serenity through strength, good mind, and righteousness. Of all these, such a person shall be Yours, because he has come fully out of the fiery test."

Gathas: Song 3

How the Demonic is More Loved

A person's value system and neural pathways take the shape of the information most absorbed, repeated, and used, and modern environments are attempting to socialize or darwinize the person to function through the agents of the demonic half of the mind more so than the angelic. To that effect, from the left, the right, the front, and the back, negative influences constantly hound the person.

Now, that doesn't mean that people are walking around all crazed. All I'm suggesting is that come the appropriate circumstances, the selfish attributes are encouraged to dominate and shape a person's awareness when they shouldn't.

The dominant elements of the built world that provoke and nurture the ugly half of the mind are the market and her offspring (the consumer culture), the collective intelligence that reinforces the market and her child, the violent and immoral dimensions of history and culture, and the illusion of the built world.

The attributes of the market that nurture the agents of the ugly are:

A) A paycheque-to-paycheque existence balanced on a line of credit, the irrational cost of living, and the inflated competitive nature of the contemporary market.

A person is forced to chase their basic needs, each person is pitted against another in their chase, and most are unable to secure their basics for a prolonged period of time. Under such inductions, a person's mind naturally forgets the collective attributes, and the mind naturally leans towards a self-centered and ugly attitude.

If a person's long-term prosperity, security, and potential to meet the basics are constantly under threat, as it is under a paycheque-to-paycheque reality and a life on credit, the mind does little but think about alleviating that threat or the mind stresses about that threat. That type of attitude naturally traps the consciousness to the ugly, and the demonic naturally restricts the beautiful of the person's duality. The mindset is what traps and the market is the catalyst.

The market coerces the mind to harbour lower level values, and the person is kept so busy by the chase that they have little time and energy to develop a higher state of awareness. The current economic circumstances do not permit most people to grow, and most people are only sanctioned to maintain an existence. And the market efforts to socialize a person to operate more so influenced by the selfish because that condition is in the benefit of the market, and those who dominate it.

That all said, I thought people entered into a social contract to create the conditions required to secure the basics for a prolonged period of time. I thought markets and societies came to be so to assist the person harness the human condition's fullest potential and to the heavens climb.

Perhaps, that was true in the beginning, but on the contemporary scene, it would seem that most have forgotten why they entered into a social contract. And ironically, markets and societies have progressed to the point where they're more able than ever to provide the basics to all people without the people having to bust their backs and exchange their minds for a paycheque-to-paycheque requiem.

B) A big piece of a person's day is eaten by a nine-to-five workday, and the majority of the person's wake time is fed to the built world in hopes of securing the basics required to live. Life is exchanged for life, and in the trade, the mind is left with little time to travel outside the dimensions of a job or occupation. After the built world's daily feeding session, the person has little time and energy to develop the angelic.

C) The popular culture, also known as the consumer culture, doesn't help the general public exercise their full potential, and it assists the market in doing so. Articulated within the blueprint, that culture readily ignores the collective and loves the agents of the selfish cognitive condition.

The agents of the selfish are given more attention by the consumer culture because those agents are the only ones that can help the market realize its full potential, and they encourage the person to indulge in the over-consumption of goods, services, and entertainment. Some of the elements of our popular culture that nurture the selfish and, consequently, neglect the collective cognitive condition are:

1. The idea of the individual before the community.

2. The many unrealistic, artificial, and conditioned beliefs and wants--beyond those that are necessities.

3. The ideas that artificially inflate and manipulate an individual's innate wants. For example, in the consumer culture, for a person to belong or to be accepted, an individual must behave a certain way, hold certain possessions, wear certain clothes, etc. What should be luxuries have become necessities if a person wishes to fulfill the innate want for belonging.

4. The idea that a person exists to please the senses and entertain the mind and body.

5. The idea that a person exists to accumulate irrational amounts of wealth and to hoard resources.

6. The idea that success is measured by the amount of material holdings and capital a person possesses.

7. Information that encourages a person to morally compromise or to engage strictly in the senses, information like that pushed by movies such as *Scarface, Godfather, American Pie, Reservoir Dogs, How to be a Player,* and *Casino.* The same can be said about television shows such as the *Sopranos, Sex in the City, Desperate Housewives, Jersey Shore, The Hills, Temptation Island, Peak Season,* and all the soap opera dramas. And music like that created by most studio gangsters and pioneered by musicians like Eazy-E and Too Short.

For the system to maintain its power, the people must never stop selfishly wanting more, and for the system to grow, the selfish wanting can never discontinue. You see, so they don't seize, the gears of the machine must be endlessly greased. To that end, the popular culture readily, and now effortlessly, attempts to breed selfish people.

What's more, the collective intelligence actually reinforces and propagates the value system created by the market. The collective intelligence expects the people to harbour the value system sold by popular culture. Those who don't conform to the collective intelligence typically suffer social marginalization and all the pain that comes with.

The violent and immoral dimensions of history and culture:

The attributes of history, popular culture, the collective intelligence, and the media that glorify and romanticize a violent ethos, especially violence disguised and unjustly carried out in the name of freedom, liberty, justice, truth, God, progress, entertainment, or success.

A glorified and romanticized violent history and culture are taught so to provide examples of when it's appropriate to act violently. More specifically, to justify war when the time comes for war, to influence the people to soldier, and to keep the middle-class fighting amongst each other and in a state of controlled conflict when there is no war to distract them. The desensitization to violence, conflict, and all that comes with it, naturally nurtures the demonic over the angelic.

Illusion of the built world:

The built world camouflages the natural world. The disappearance of the natural realm from a person's mind restricts an individual from experiencing and absorbing the information nature has to offer.

Interaction with the natural realm is extremely important because the person springs from that realm. It would be reasonable to assume that the answers or clues to a person's true purpose would be there.

If an individual did truthfully translate and reflect the natural realm, the person would naturally grow to function through the collective cognitive condition. That is, when the person isn't attempting to satisfy their physiological needs or defend the self.

A person's value system takes the shape of the information most absorbed, repeated, and used, and it would appear that modern environments are conditioning and socializing the person to function through the ugly half of the mind more so than the collective cognitive condition.

The built world attempts to train the mind to ignore the collective cognitive condition, and it does that by keeping a person busy chasing after wants, by keeping a person's awareness absorbed in pleasing the senses (during the downtime), by giving a person directionless purposes like a want for a larger house or a shinier car, by separating a person from nature, by coercing a person to live paycheque-to-paycheque and subsidized by a line of credit, and by desensitizing the mind to violence and conflict.

Unnatural Evolution

When I suggest that the system attempts to provoke the demonic half to dominate, I'm implying that the machine efforts to condition the ugly to override the communications of the beautiful. Come the appropriate stimulant, the mind is taught to devalue the communications of the beautiful in favour of the demonic.

The law and social acceptance seem to be the two dominant forces that keep the selfish in check, but if the appropriate stimulant and the two silently intersect, ugly thoughts have a beastly potential to morph into actions.

The intersection of an appropriate stimulant, and the disappearance of the two that dominantly keep the ugly from acting, can induce the mind to entertain the communications produced by the agents of the demonic half--especially if the ugly is nurtured. For example, if a person is in an angry state of mind and wishes to hurt a particular someone, and there are no immediate consequences, the person is more likely to act on their state of mind.

The natural evolution of the individual is tampered with. Without the intrusion, most people would grow to scold the influences of the ugly through the agents of the mind's beautiful portion. That's not to say that the built world does not communicate information with a beautiful intention. However, just enough is indoctrinated so to give the angelic a minimal presence and to keep the people from turning cities to ashes. For an example of what I'm talking about, take a look at the newspapers. The majority of the news consists of sensational and negative substance like murder, corruption, terrorism, sex, and so on, and only a small percentage of the substance is dedicated to positive information. The same phenomenon is evident in all the other popular mediums. The ugly half has infected popular culture.

It should be noted that the demonic condition harbours negative emotions such as fear, anger, and disgust, and the different popular mediums constantly provoke a person's negative emotions to reinforce the overall selfish half of the mind. The provocation instils a negative/dark aura that can autonomously pull on and provoke negative thoughts and experiences. Feelings such as fear, anger, and disgust emanate specific vibrations and those vibrations attract the like. More importantly, when those types of vibrations are produced, the person isn't creating positive vibrations like those triggered by love, and the

206

person isn't compelling a positive resonance. Nor is a person producing a state necessary to strengthen the magnetic field they emanate. Everything earthly resonates a magnetic field, and the stronger it is, the better the vitality and health. Thoughts, words, feelings, and actions, created under the influence of the selfish condition, damage an individual's magnetic field. The angelic half of the mind has the opposite effect.

The selfish condition is a dominant source of a person's suffering, not only for vibrational and magnetic reasons, but also because that half recognizes and validates suffering.

Self-governing principles taught by the family and religion are also dominant influences that keep a person from overindulging in the lesser half of the mind, but they must be taught. Another influence that provides a beautiful persuasion is the soul. The idea of the soul is addressed in an upcoming article.

The machine synthetically efforts to strengthen the selfish of the mind's dichotomy, and if not for the unnatural interference, the beautiful wouldn't be so easily overridden and the ugly would rarely show its face. That is, when the person's physiological needs are secure and satisfied.

"I swear by the time, most surely man is in loss, except those who believe and do good, and enjoin on each other truth, and enjoin on each other patience."--(Qur'an 103:1-3)

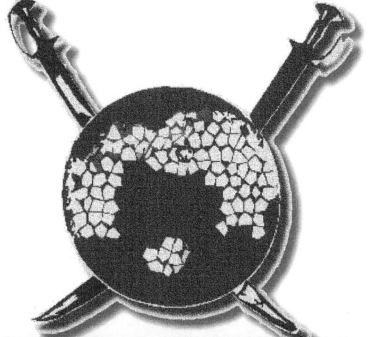

If possible it is for God to have enemies, then those enemies must be the agents of the ugly.

The Consequences of the Ugly

The selfish cognitive condition can become a demonic possession, and it can blind the "I" from seeing another's invisible existence. Under its influence, an individual's thoughts rarely travel further than the individual they inhibit-- recognition and validation of another's metaphysical condition diminishes. A person's perception of the self and other people becomes different, different compared to an empathetic or compassionate state of consciousness.

All the wrong that a person is capable of such as lying, cheating, stealing, adultery, promiscuity, bullying, injuring another, murder, exploitation, slander, and greed originate from the selfish half of the mind. Fiendishly, the ugly blurs the influence of the beautiful like the smog that hides the shine of the stars at night.

The same is true when the beautiful is the mind's lord, but in the opposite sense, and the angelic hides the darkness by emanating light. When the beautiful is the dominant condition, ugly thoughts remain just that and demonic thoughts rarely enter the thought process. If they do, the influences of the beautiful are typically able to suppress them.

It's more than obvious that of the two conditions the angelic is in the benefit of civilized nations. The angelic keeps the selfish in check. In the process, it also attracts beautiful thoughts, actions, and experiences. But for some reason, it doesn't appear to be the dominant cognitive condition nurtured by civilized nations.

"The mind controlled by the sinful nature is death, but the mind controlled by the Spirit is life and peace."--(Romans 8:6)

211

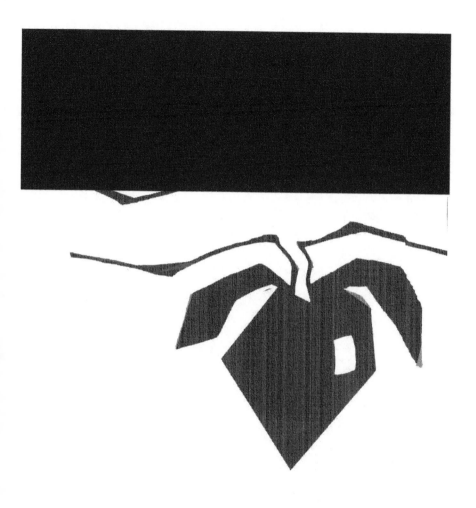

Not only does the selfish cognitive condition harbour the potential to influence the person to morally, ethically, and legally compromise, the selfish condition also alienates. The selfish alienates the person from the unborn, their First Mother, their neighbour, the community as a whole, and the suffering of the less fortunate.

Perhaps, we're Godless. Perhaps, we're mentally challenged. Or maybe, just maybe, somewhere along the line of our civil evolution, we muzzled the good within the person.

<u>Remorseless</u>

Since the first time I was witness, I've asked myself the question, "What motivates a person to hurt another?" I've asked myself that because I've seen many people--some close and some not so, deliberately hurt another. The means and reasons usually differed, but the ends were always similar. Pain was placed on another human being.

You might be surprised to find that victims are both the injurer and the injured, and the first is a victim in the sense that they were unable to control the balance of information within them. You see, certain changes take place within the injurer before they gain the motivation to injure another. Before a person gains the motivation to hurt another person, the better parts of the mind typically silence--parts such as empathy and compassion, and the ugly simultaneously begins to influence. Within that type of mindset, an individual is at a high risk of offending and it's easy for one's thoughts to justify hurting another's existence.

It's easy to hurt another's existence when the better parts of the mind are swayed into detention and the agents of the demonic are active. The ugly is characteristically provoked into action when a want or a belief is threatened or unsatisfied. Unfortunately, our popular culture conditions far too many unrealistic wants and beliefs.

When the ugly half of the mind is active, a temporary separation of the man and the demon can be the consequence, and all separations are temporary. The mindset ideal for placing pain, in most, is a temporary setting. Shortly after the stimulation leaves, the mindset proceeds.

Every person holds within him or her the cognitive agents that can influence thoughts and actions to place pain on another. Every person has the potential. However, every individual also has the potential to prevent the self from hurting another. A person can prevent their mind from hurting another by constructing and nurturing a beautiful value system, by creating beliefs that

215

allow a person to understand how the mind works, and by constructing values that suppress the ugly of the mind's condition.

Potential victims are all but those who attempt to prevent the downward slide, and modern environments don't intentionally instruct their occupants on how to resist. Instead, they love the selfish cognitive condition more so than the collective. Just as a U.S Marine and a NASA Engineer need instruction, conditioning, and reinforcement to be, a person also requires the same before the person can dominantly function through the beautiful half of the mind's duality.

"Man's nature is naturally good just as water naturally flows downward."--Mencius

The Truest Me

The manufactured world presents selfishness as a phenomenon of nature like a thunderstorm. But the truth is that the degeneration is more so constructed, and since we're translations, it's clear that the agents of the collective consciousness were silenced. Like seeds sowed and forgotten.

Nonetheless, ancient wisdom which suggests that it's the attributes of the angelic that are to dominantly influence, can't be denied. The proof of that position is within the children.

Initially, their minds are governed by the collective parts of the person. That is, when the mind's innate wants are quiet. If the true nature of the person were selfish, then children would be selfish. But as we all know, children are very much the opposite.

Children are very much angelic, and for the most part, that only changes when they learn to function differently. However, that doesn't mean that the beautiful can be forever silenced. I've seen the most selfish of people perform acts of kindness.

Children are very much angelic, but for some reason, during the infant years, the human condition naturally enters a temporary selfish phase. The child temporarily thinks like a king or a queen... above debate and consequence... always absolute and conclusive... and everything is theirs and no one else's. It's possible that an individual is designed to enter the temporary selfish phase so to survive nature. Nonetheless, it doesn't make sense to harness that potential.

Most people are born to be kind, but some individuals, somewhere along the line of their Darwinized life, adapted to allow the selfish to dominate.

The manufactured world presents selfishness as a phenomenon of nature like a thunderstorm. But the truth is the degeneration is more so constructed, and since we're translations, it's clear the agents of the collective consciousness were silenced. Like seeds sowed and forgotten.

The God-Consciousness and the consumer culture are on opposite ends of the spectrum. At one end stands the ugly, and at the other, the beautiful.

God Conscious Citizen

The dark parts of the world are unnaturally authoritarian--unnatural in the sense that the built world nurtures the dark around and within while neglecting The Great Void.

The built world attempts to condition people to ignore the invisible, and simultaneously, it efforts to train people to care little for the whole. Instead, bred was love for the individual. And instead, conditioned was the desire to house and chase artificially inflated wants and not those that carry higher value.

And I guess it's easy not to care. It's easy not to care about that which isn't taught. The human condition is designed to absorb information and translate. Our metaphysical and physical motions are based on the beliefs and the ideas learned, and the parts of the mind nurtured by the environments. Regrettably, modern environments do not teach the truest beliefs. Instead, they instil the need for unnecessary things--worldly and fleeting, they numb the person to the world's hungry, and they breed the mind blind to the community, humanity, morality, the spirit, and The Absolute Reality.

Bred to be... bred to be... bred to reinforce the status quo and provide sweat to fuel the spiritually alienated machinery.

If we were raised different, we would want more--more for our spiritual selves. But "more for" would mean less for the few, and it's the few who temporarily benefit from what the modern woman and man have become. We should've been raised as God Conscious Citizens but we were raised as something else.

That something else can be categorized as a consumer. More often than not, a consumer refers to an individual who spends the majority of their wake time working toward, using, maintaining, purchasing, disposing of, and thinking about basics needs, products, or services.

Now, when a consumer isn't engaged in the above and time is idle, the consumer is typically busy working to please and entertain the senses (pleasure motivates). Along that line, the attitude of a consumer primarily creates selfish beliefs and wants, chiefly influences the person to satisfy the self, and nurtures the selfish cognitive condition.

A God Conscious Citizen, on the other hand, views the world differently. For example, they, in thought, word, and action attempt to behave ethically and morally. They love and selflessly serve the people and the community. They advocate truth and equality (for the sake of truth and equality). They work to improve the built world so it can improve the person. They appreciate the Essence of God within the self and in every entity. They seek absolute knowledge and higher reasoning. They love The Eternal and meditate/ contemplate/ praise The Great Void. They focus their consciousness so to discover the principles that govern such as heaven, hell, karma, the chakras, and death. They live content, virtuous, and egoless. They work to uncover The Name and the Word within the person. And for any sins, they earnestly ask for forgiveness.

A God Conscious Citizen creates wants and beliefs framed by the above stipulations and those related. Not surprisingly, such an individual nurtures and functions through the collective cognitive condition.

Now, if a person wishes to become a Super God Conscious Citizen, she or he is required to levitate above the selfish condition and the beautiful half. An achievement few people accomplish, and only with the help of The Great Architect.

The market attempts to create the consumer as opposed to the God Conscious Citizen because the first maintains the status quo and helps the market grow. A God Conscious Citizen isn't in the benefit of the market. If that type of person constituted the majority, the market would regress because people would be spending less, and the type of values that empower the contemporary elite would no longer be prevalent.

By structuring the information an individual absorbs and transforms into wants and beliefs, the human mind can be guided to want almost anything. Most people will become the information they experience and that can be used to a community's advantage. Just as a soldier is taught to soldier, a God Conscious Citizen can also be moulded, and just as a consumer is influenced to consume things, the person can be influenced to become a Godly Citizen.

We could've been raised differently but the powers that be attempt to raise us senseless. We were bred to overindulge and over-consumer and act as if the act made divine sense.

Instead of teaching the people to restrain the demonic, our popular culture and our collective intelligence do the opposite. Simultaneously, they both invest little in ideas and practices of self-control and cognitive development.

Cognitive development isn't encouraged and to develop the mind is to allow the angelic half of the mind's dichotomy to create thoughts and actions. Thoughts and actions constructed with the beautiful as the architect are thoughts and actions considered God conscious.

The Darwin Deception

For the last few sections, we've discussed the various shortcomings of the socio-political agenda, and its impact on the person. In this article, we'll discuss how science also contributes.

Industrialism, through science, attempts to neutralize the God Conscious by popularizing such ideas as the Theory of Evolution presented by Darwin. Unfortunately, the theory is like the flat earth assumption, and we all know that the earth is very much rounded.

Many people seem to believe that the human being evolved from the ape. For the most part, they believe what they do because the popular culture has taught them to believe their ancestors are primates. But the theory is just a theory and necessary numbers are missing from the equation. Without those numbers, the Theory of Evolution is inconclusive.

The premise presented by Darwin isn't complete, and the theory is missing pieces when applied to the human being. For example, the leap from pre-human to human would require more than one missing link. It would require dozens for the transition to have taken place. The same is true for every transitional stage presented by the theory.

The multiple jumps detailed by Darwin are just too drastic, and the theory doesn't account for the happenings. Besides, none of the many missing links (transitional species) Darwin's theory suggests have been recovered.

The many missing links required for Darwin's theory to work are yet to be discovered. To throw another wrench in the equation, authors such as Michael A. Cremo and Richard L. Thompson advocate that the different skeletal evidence discovered and attributed to the various stages of the human evolution are evidence of different and distinct species--species that no longer exist. Not only that, the two suggest archaeologists have discovered human skeletons that date much further back than what mainstream archaeology tells the world. Darwin's theory doesn't account for those discoveries.

Cremo and Thompson further imply that the discoveries of these skeletal remains are not popular because the archaeological establishment, led by the

Smithsonian, are purposely destroying and hiding evidence that doesn't align with Darwin's Theory of Evolution.

The skeletal evidence presented, and the supposed skeletal proof hypothesised, are not the only elements that discredit Darwin's presumption. Several other arguments can also be recruited to deny the idea, for example, the human condition's ability to grow hair, a person's skin pigmentation, and the existence of apes.

According to Darwin, people who live in very hot regions of the world shouldn't be able to grow too much body hair, and people who live in colder regions of the planet should be covered in the stuff. However, that isn't the case. The indigenous peoples of Northern Canada have very little hair, and a strong percentage of people from Punjab have more body hair than the Northern Indigenous Canadians.

"Sunburn" is another good example. By now, people should've adapted to live under the sun. The skin should not burn.

And I thought the supposed ancestors of the human couldn't survive earthly environments. Darwin suggests that the ape's inability to cope with the environment forced the evolution to a human. But if that was so, then why are apes still around? An adaptation is evident but a transition from one species to another isn't.

At this point, I think it's important to mention that with the introduction of the industrial revolution also came a crusade to eliminate the idea of God from popular thought. The idea of God, and the companion beliefs, do not compliment the dominant ideas of an industrial society and the culture it facilitates. The idea of God actually prevents industrialism from growing, and the notion of A Great Architect tends to free a person's mind from the physical plain of existence, under that impression, an individual will value more than just consumption, entertainment, and sensations.

Deceived by Darwin and those who backed his notion, the elite ruling class who benefitted from the dominance of an industrial society, Darwin's presumptions were presented as an absolute truth and nothing but, but "buts" there are.

228

Interestingly, Darwin was initially the co-author of the Theory of Evolution, and Alfred Russel Wallace was the other individual who introduced the theory to the world. Wallace was about to present the idea to the world solo but Darwin, who was independently and simultaneously developing the theory, wanted in on the debut of the ape to person myth. Needless-to-say, Wallace accepted his request. However, the name "Wallace" is no longer associated with the ape-man theory and he's no longer associated to it by choice. Wallace divorced himself from the idea.

That all said, this doesn't mean that the theories of Creation the different religions present are without fault. However, all of them converge on one point I wholly agree with; God created life.

Science should be admired but not when it pedals half-conclusive ideas as truth. I am a child of God, not pond goo, and Darwinism is the new flat earth.

Dawkins' Assumption

Agnostics such as Dawkins not only use the corruption of religions to stroke the idea that there is no God, they rely on the argument that the consciousness is a side-effect of evolution.

The proposal suggests that the consciousness came after the human body and not before it. Supposedly, the conscious component of the person eventually developed to help the human survive the wild, and continued to evolve as interactions with the environment became more and more complex. However, that hypothesis can't be proven, and it relies heavily on Darwin's Theory of Evolution, which also can't be established.

Science is further unable to prove wrong the assertions of the holy. The saints were and are adamant that the true "I" isn't the physical, and the body is just a vessel the "I" temporarily experiences--moving on after the body ceases. However, science can present the fact that the consciousness detaches from the body at death. But that's where mainstream science stops. Their methods and tools do not allow them to go further. The detachment from the body is the first step in the transition. Mainstream science isn't yet capable of examining the proceeding, or for that matter, the true essence of the consciousness, independent of the body's influences.

Mainstream science is still young but considers itself a seasoned veteran.

Flicker

The Age of Iron this is as described by the Eastern ancients. The three legs to the table of religion are broken, and wickedness is like a shadow, allusive with its intentions.

Wickedness surrounds our everyday motions, and as most have witnessed, wickedness is very much within us. As Pandora did, we allow the wicked to enter the realm of the living.

Fortunately, the Universe isn't unaware of this. Mysteriously, the Universe is conscious, every so often, reintroducing moral intelligence when morality begins to thin--reintroducing moral intelligence when the ugly half of the mind's duality dominates human motions.

The person has the potential to give rise to the wicked within and sometimes civilizations evolve to accidentally harness that potential. When civilizations do step too far out of bounds, the Universe appears to intervene to give an example. An example of how the person should be living.

The Universe has intervened numerous times, and from a pool of infinite choices, the Universe intervened and created the pious like Jesus, Buddha, Mohammad, and Nanak.

Against all odds, they rose to illuminate. Against all the secular forces they stood, survived, and gave wisdom. Through them, by intervening, the Universe chose to answer the most resolute questions--What is our purpose and how should we live? To all the God sent, thank you for demonstrating the beautiful half of the mind's condition.

"To enjoy good health, to bring true happiness to one's family, to bring peace to all, one must first discipline and control one's own mind. If a man can control his mind he can find the way to Enlightenment, and all wisdom and virtue will naturally come to him."--Buddha

Good Deeds

We all seem so caught up in the "he said--she said" drama, counting loose change, and the chase to fill the home with worldly things that most have forgotten to fill the home that be. And the only way to fill that home is by accomplishing good deeds--in thought, word, and action.

When I write "the home that be" I refer to the soul, and from my experiences, the built world rarely allows the person to nurture the invisible. Instead, it keeps the person's mind and time so busy chasing needless desires and sensory pleasures that the person eventually forgets to love their better part.

Needless desires and sensory pleasures distract the person from loving their better part, and the best method to overcome the distractions is by way of accomplishing deeds deemed good.

Good deeds are the only that fill the home that be because good deeds nurture the parts of the mind that allow the mind to love and develop the invisible. It's like a math formula without the numbers.

You see, good deeds nurture the better half of the mind, including the feelings attached to that condition, because good deeds force the mind to use the better half and its agents. More importantly, as with any part of the mind repeatedly used, it can eventually grow to dominate the decision-making process, and the better half can potentially influence without having to be accessed.

That is the objective, to merge the better half with a person's character. At which point, the beautiful half of the mind will automatically fill the home that be and automatically develop "the Light" within (the soul).

To fill the home that be is to give the soul attention so the soul can influence, and every time the mind's better half is used, a person gives attention to the soul and the soul grows in strength, just like a muscle of the body grows when exercised.

But why spend the time and the energy developing the mind and the soul when there are so many worldly wonders to be had?

It's important to develop the mind and the soul because the body is just a temporary stage. The invisible within the person is the only with the potential

234

to enter the next phase. Accordingly, it's very plausible the invisible can enter that stage developed or underdeveloped.

"To do good deeds is the best rosary. Chant on the beads within your heart, and it shall go along with you. ||1||"--(Sri Guru Granth Sahib Ji, ang 1134)

The Mind and the Soul

For the sake of convenience, I've decided to call the place where thoughts are projected, Thought Energy. Thought Energy is the "I" in this reality; the arena where we consciously dream, imagine, anticipate, build, converse, question, want, perceive, see, taste, smell, hear, think, feel, judge, plan, infer, administer, and evaluate. All conscious thoughts and actions are mapped there.

When creating, perceiving, imagining, etc., Thought Energy is receiving and/or accessing information--no matter how insignificant and off the radar. The two sources from which information is sent or accessed through and from are the soul and the mind. In the sending or accessing of information, either external information stimulated motion, internal information activated without stimulation, or Thought Energy behaved introspective.

There are two mega-units of information within the person that influence a person's thoughts, the mind and the soul. (The mind is fixed to the brain, and the brain is tied to the body). These mega-units are composed of smaller units of information. For example, within the mega-unit that is the mind, you will find units of information coined value configurations. Value configurations contain learned information such as beliefs, knowledge, and expectations. They also develop to govern innate units such as anger. A value configuration linked to an innate unit contains information learned about that innate unit-- information such as how to interpret the communication of the innate unit, when to allow its influence to communicate to the place thoughts are determined, and the general concept of the intrinsic.

The mega-unit that is the soul consists of, for example, the units of information termed the Chakras. All units within the soul are innate.

Thought Energy, in most cases, is born more so influenced by the information and operations of the soul. However, the influence of the soul can grow to become a secondary source. This occurs when the mind, and the value configuration that governs Thought Energy, evolve to understand itself as the lone source of information able to communicate to Thought Energy.

The above state of mind is the consequence of the selfish cognitive condition having more importance than the beautiful half of the mind's duality. Under that state of awareness, layers of externally experienced information will bury the influences of the soul.

For some reason, the selfish naturally blocks the influence of the soul, whereas, the beautiful naturally allows the soul's influences to flow to Thought Energy.

The Soul
The soul is the person's life force; it gives energy for the electrons and the neutrons to fire and genes to become genes. The soul, as mentioned, is also an agent with the ability to communicate to the place where thoughts are mapped, and like the mind, it too is home to innate information. Likewise, value configurations (beliefs), constructed and housed by the mind, can eventually grow to mediate the soul's innate information.

Unfortunately, constructed knowledge, in the form of value configurations, can misinterpret the communications of the soul. The sensation of the soul's innate communication will be felt but the mind might associate that sensation with the constructed idea of that impression.

The innate units of the soul encourage such happenings as higher reasoning, empathy, and oneness. They can be categorized under the following three headings: innate wants, units of manipulation, and units of knowledge. The innate wants of the soul behave like those of the mind; however, they can be left unsatisfied without threatening the survival of the human condition.

1. Innate wants
    a) Higher reasoning: a want for absolute truth and a want for life purposes beyond the secular.
    b) Oneness: a want for sharing, belonging, unconditional love, universal oneness, and God.

2. Units of Manipulation
    a) Empathy: sympathy and empathy are often confused, and empathy is to feel what another is feeling whereas sympathy is to understand what another is feeling.

    b) The tenth gate / the mind's eye.

3. Units of Knowledge

237

a) If each person does house memories from a past existence, then that information is within the soul.

b) The Eastern saints suggest that all absolute knowledge of existence is stored within each human condition. It's a matter of accessing that information. The Chakra units are examples of units of knowledge within the soul. The information within the Chakras can be stimulated to influence, and that through meditation. The second volume details a meditative technique to motivate the Chakras to communicate.

c) The formula to merge with The Great Architect is hidden in the soul. As is the celestial vibration, the Word, that produces the state of being known as nirvana.

The Mind

The mind, home to units of information capable of communicating to the place thoughts and actions are mapped, is a phenomenon of one's brain, and each person's brain functions in relation to their unique genetic make-up. William Wright, in his book, *Born that Way* (1998), tells that *"genes influence not just physical traits but personalities, temperaments, behavioral patterns, personal idiosyncrasies, the quirks and fallacies that make each person unique."*

Likewise, although each mind carries out its function differently, the function of every mind is the same: to seek, gather, interpret, hold, process, and communicate information.

> *"The brain ... is an information-processing system. And this fact about the brain is ... 'intrinsic'. It is just a fact about biology that the brain functions to process information."*--(John Searle, *The Rediscovery of the Mind.* 1992)

In accordance, the mind of an adult houses two general types of information, innate and constructed. Innate information is with only a genetic link like aggression or appetite. Constructed information is learned from outside the human condition.

The mind's innate units such as anger produce innate information. The innate units of the mind are categorized under the following three headings: **innate**

238

wants, units of manipulation, and **units of Aura**. All are eventually mediated by learned values and all are facilitated by the brain.

The second type of information housed within the mind is constructed and that type is influenced to become by both innate and environmental information. Consider them an amalgamation of the person and the environment. The constructed units, eventually housed by the mind, are value configurations (beliefs), **units of thought, decoded units of information**, and **units of memory**.

When creating, perceiving, imagining, etc., Thought Energy is receiving and/or accessing information--no matter how insignificant and off the radar. The two sources from which information is sent or accessed through and from are the soul and the mind. Of the two conditions facilitated by the mind, the beautiful allows the information within the soul to communicate to Thought Energy, and the greater the influence of the angelic, the greater the influence of the soul. The other half of the mind only blocks the invisible's communications.

The Home in Me

So many people chase to fill their home with worldly things;
so many sweat and stress but forget to fill the home they be.

Life Purpose

If every individual is with a unique and divine purpose, then that purpose must be within each person. For the uniqueness within the person is the only uniqueness the person is privy to. Everything outside the human condition is without that potential. Why? Because everything outside can be applied to another.

Each person's unique purpose is to conquer the mind and to allow the soul and the beautiful to dominantly influence the time and space of thought. Although the end goal is the same for every person, each individual can only reach the ideal state by finding and traveling their own unique road, and by conquering their own unique dispositions. Dispositions innate, and if a mind is unguided, dispositions randomly conditioned by the built world.

In this case, the word "disposition" refers to the agents and the beliefs capable of suppressing or contradicting the influence of the collective cognitive condition, and by extension, the soul.

Each person has ugly agents and ugly beliefs that influence to different degrees, and their influences, combined together, create each person's unique starting point (dynamic).

Although the end goal is the same, each can only get there through their own unique means and by conquering the unique manner in which the ugly half of the mind's community influences the creation of thought, word, and action.

Every religion I've looked at stressed the importance of conquering the demonic and allowing the angelic to reign over thoughts and actions. To do that, a person must travel through the self, and the inward journey is a solitary one--no other person can accompany you there. However, The Great Architect is in all spaces and interspaces. The Lord can help. Through the Ultimate Teacher, the Holy Spirit, God can guide you to conquer the self.

> *"In the same way, the Spirit helps us in our weakness. We do not know what we ought to pray for, but the Spirit himself intercedes for us through wordless groans."*--(Romans 8:26)

"But the Advocate, the Holy Spirit, whom the Father will send in my name, will teach you all things and will remind you of everything I have said to you."--(John 14:26)

Instinctually, the human condition is aware of its higher purpose. When the better half isn't dominating the construction of thoughts and actions, uncomfortable thoughts and feelings seem to surface, such as purposelessness, isolation, sadness, and discomfort. These feelings are indicators like the seatbelt beeper annoyingly reminding you to strap yourself in. Like the car, we too were purposely designed with instructional mechanisms, so to remind us of the boundaries we should be operating within.

If every individual is with a unique and divine purpose, then that purpose must be within each person. For the uniqueness within the person is the only uniqueness the person is privy to. Everything outside the human condition is without that potential. Why? Because everything outside can be applied to another.

My Church Be Where I Be

I chase only immortality;
enslavement of the ugly half of my mind's duality,
such as lust, anger, the selfish ego, attachment, and greed.
To conquer them is to live in harmony.
To conquer them is to conquer the living.

I Am

For a person to intentionally conquer their disposition, and for a person to identify their unique starting point, an individual is required to understand the self. The best method to discover the self is by critically, truthfully, and patiently evaluating the self. With time, a person will develop their own ideas of the self. Simultaneously, a person should study religion and the Liberal Arts (the stuff a good university teaches), and talk to someone in the know. After which, an individual should modify their own understanding. Eventually, a person will come to understand their unique disposition and the wisdom required to conquer it. Oh, and don't be afraid to pray to the Great Helper. If God's Spirit sees it fit, all truths can be revealed in an instant.

We are spiritual beings having a human experience and not vice versa. Think of the self as a pilot, and the body, with its components such as the mind, as the jet.

In the Same Boat

Gold, diamonds, and platinum; pop cans, loose change, and cardboard, whatever the lifestyle might be, all are without purpose if all fail to conquer the mind's duality.

- All are without purpose if the mind blows in the wind and if death is understood as the end.

- All are without purpose if detached from the higher mind and if the mind's eye is blind.

- All are without purpose if the soul isn't developed and if the ugly envelops.

- All are without purpose if they can't see the separation, the separation of the ugly and the angelic.

No person is with a higher purpose if he or she isn't striving to love the beautiful consciousness, and the angelic can only be loved by using it. Only then, is there a distinction between two. Only then, is there purpose to me or you.

It doesn't matter if you're a beggar or a judge because both are of the same caste. There is only a distinction between the two if one lives through the beautiful half. But it's probably better to be a judge with a higher state of mind than a beggar who's developed the beauty within. Simply because every person must meet his or her natural basic needs, and it's quicker and easier to meet them with a fat bank account than by begging.

You can be a doctor, a waiter, or a judge. You can be a beggar, a junkie, or a thug. In the end, it doesn't matter under which title a person struggles. All are of the same caste if all are detached from the beautiful half.

Chapter 3
Love

"...This wondrous painting is now the problem. Forget this picture and focus your consciousness on the Painter. || 12 ||" Ang 340 of Sri Guru Granth Sahib Ji (a passage by the famous Muslim poet, Kabeer)

The Key to God's Door

There are many names given to the one Lord and Master. However, it isn't the given name that matters but the state of consciousness when contemplating that name. Likewise, remembrance without the appropriate state of consciousness is as fruitless as idol worship. That said; remembrance without a spiritual gateway or guide is almost as worthless.

Opportunely, the consciousness of Jesus, Buddha, Nanak, Mohammad, and many more are still in the air. Use any of them as your gateway and meditate on The One. Meditate on The One's universal attributes. Contemplate, contemplate, and you will find the Light within and The Eternal.

To help with your journey, daily nurture the influences of the mind that allow for, and shape, the consciousness to perceive the Light within and The Supreme Light--influences of the mind such as compassion, truth, contentment, love, and humility. Not only that, neglect those that prevent the consciousness from perceiving--influences such as anger, lust, attachment, ego, and greed.

Under such inductions, the vibrations created by thoughts and feelings are in tune with celestial vibrations. The concept of vibrations is discussed in much more detail in volume two, and understanding them is an important step on the staircase of spiritual progression. The idea suggests that loving thoughts and feelings naturally bring forth loving experiences. The happening is an absolute, like the relationship of a circle's circumference to its diameter. Love will always equal love.

"'Love the Lord your God with all your heart and with all your soul and with all your mind and with all your strength.' The second is this: 'Love your neighbor as yourself.' There is no commandment greater than these."--(Mark 12:30-31)

I Forgot

I fell in love with the fruits of the maker's labour
but I forgot to love the maker.

The Road to Success

A mountain is a hill and an ocean a pond. My legs are those of a giant and as are my arms. A year is a day and 100 miles a few blocks. But with no love for and from, a velvet ant I am, lost on a branch, in the forests of the Amazon.

In the mindset of a loving child rests the path to our salvation.

Playing Detective

Nothing in the physical realm can provide a constant induction. No noun. No verb. Fortunately, only half the Universe the physical is, and now-a-days, I look to the invisible for an unbreakable stimulant.

My hypothesis is: Fallacies of the built world corrupt the innocent love. In today's days, only God's Light can unconditionally give back that innocence.

I believe that the unbreakable love I seek, a love for and a love from, rests with The Eternal Commander and Chief. I believe The Formless One will never break the induction, unless of course, I make the disconnection.

Love for and from The Lord is the only permanent love in the whole of existence. Endeavour I do to experience, and not just in thought but also in feeling. Thoughts and feelings are different, and each can be considered a unique language. To love The Lord in belief and thought is the first step. The second is to feel that love. Feelings produce vibrations and the vibration of love resonates with the Essence of God.

So, love The One as a child loves; with no conditions, without the obstacle that is constructed love, with complete focus, and through pure innocence. Experience then, say the saints, The Lord's Glance of Greatness.

Playing detective.

When a person is angry, he or she will perceive the world differently than if he or she were in love. When a person is angry, it's difficult to understand the world of love. The same is true of the better half of the mind. It's a reality that's difficult to understand when the mind's eye is constantly looking through the ugly.

A limited perception of reality is taken when the ugly governs thoughts and actions, and not many were taught of the demonic limitation. Allow the angelic to dominantly influence and experience a life without blinders. Love the beautiful half of the mind and increase your love for The Eternal.

Metaphysical Dopamine

In search of love, in search of dopamine,
impulses drove me to love a dozen ladies.
In search of love, in search of peace,
impulses drove me to indulge in the temporary.

Needless to say, I stumbled.
And needless to say, I lost love a dozen times.
A dozen times I was cracked.
A dozen busted backs.
Bit by bit, broken.

Now-a-days, rebuilt I am and back at it again;
searching for dopamine.
However, ambitions are different.
I've learned from the reconfigurations,
and nowhere an unbreakable love be.
That is, nowhere in the physical,
the Universe that's visible,
is there a link that will outlast the body.

Rebuilt I be, underneath the machine, searching for metaphysical dopamine.

Love
Be Loved
Live

Love God and be a God Conscious Citizen. In God's Mercy, the Lord will send the Spirit. God's Spirit truthfully teaches, and the Spirit can give The Name of God while activating the Word within. The Word's resonance allows the "I" to experience the absolute reality. That experience can bestow salvation--union with The Great Architect, on any living thing. A permanent love, in the truest sense, can be achieved.

Appendix A: Attempted Genocide

The Sikh descendants were once a sovereign people within an internationally recognized sovereign nation, and that sovereignty was taken when the British destroyed the Sikh homeland. More important, before the creation of the Sikh nation-state and after her dismantlement, it's been the agenda of the Indian ruling class to decimate the Sikh nation.

The post-independence Indian Government has attempted to destroy the Sikh culture. The four principle reasons they've attempted to do so are:

1) To prevent the Sikh people from realizing their right to self-determination.

2) To prevent the Sikh people from realizing the strength of their collective power and philosophy.

3) To prevent the Sikhs from reclaiming their homeland.

4) And to undermine the Sikh philosophy which contradicts the dominant caste system centered Indian philosophy. That said, the argument can be made that they've almost succeeded. Today, the Sikh homeland--Punjab--is in ruin.

Many parts of the Sikh homeland are near a century behind the developed world, even though Punjab generates enough wealth for that not to be so. The Sikh homeland is behind the developed world because the Indian Governments lacked and lack the initiative to improve the conditions of the Sikh people. And let's not forget that the governments of India are extremely brutish and corrupt. Punjab could be as developed as any province in Canada or as the most developed state in India. However, post-independent India has actively worked to create intolerable social, political, and economic conditions within Punjab. Those who stood against their activities were labelled terrorists.

For example, in 1984, with the assistance of the British and the Russian Government, on the anniversary of the martyrdom of Guru Arjan,[1] the Indian army attacked the Golden Temple Complex. They attacked the complex under the guise that they were hunting so-called terrorists. In the process, they burned the Sikh Reference Library,[2] used artillery to blast holes through the Golden Temple, and murdered innocent women and children.[3] They were in the temple complex to attend the anniversary of the martyrdom of Guru Arjan.

> *"A singer at the Golden Temple, Harcharan Singh Ragi, his wife and their young daughter came out of their quarters near the information office on June 6 afternoon. They witnessed the killings of hundreds of people, including women, and would themselves have been shot if a commander had not taken pity on their young daughter who fell at his feet begging him to spare her parents' lives."[4]*

> *"A woman school teacher, Ranbir Kaur, witnessed the shooting of another group of 150 persons whose hands had been tied behind their backs with their own turbans."[5]*

> *"Children were lined up and shot in the Golden Temple by army officials."[6]*

With destruction of the Reference Library, hundreds of paintings, rare books, relics, hukamnamas, and newspapers stemming back to 1876 were turned to ashes. Tens-of-thousands of books were destroyed. And over two-thousand manuscripts of Guru Granth Sahib Ji perished.

The Indian Government claims that they attacked the Golden Temple Complex to neutralize so-called terrorists who were inside the Complex. However, the case has been made that other means were available instead of attacking the Golden Temple, the holiest place of the Sikhs, on a holy day. The case has also been made that the Indian Government attacked the Golden Temple not to neutralize the so-called terrorists but to strike fear into the minds of all Sikhs. They were attempting to send a message to the Sikh people. If the Sikhs act-up, they will be punished. That would explain why they executed innocent women and children. That would explain why they burned rare manuscripts. That would explain why they attacked the most sacred symbol of the Sikhs on a sacred day. And that would explain why they also attacked other Sikh Gurudawaras.

The Indian Government wanted to intimidate the Sikhs because the Sikhs were questioning the corrupt manner in which the Indian Government was administering the affairs of Punjab. The Sikhs were demanding better social, economic, religious, and political conditions within the land of a million martyrs. Several of the demands are outlined in the Anandpur Resolution of 1973.

Now, even though the initiatives were smaller in scope, the attack on the Golden Temple Complex wasn't the first hostile act the Indian Government is guilty of. They initiated the campaign of intimidation several years prior.

For several years before the attack on the Golden Temple Complex, the Indian Government tortured, murdered, harassed, and falsely imprisoned dozens upon dozens of Sikhs. Individuals such as Amarjeet Singh Daheru, Baljeet Singh Sultanpur, Kashmir Singh Ladhwal, and Bhola Singh were all executed in fake police encounters. The institution that is Punjab Police was the principle goon who applied the immoral campaign of intimidation. As reported by *"Night and Day News"*, 2013, Punjab Police Officer, Surjit Singh, confessed to unjustly killing over 83 Sikhs. He further implicates numerous other officers. Jaswant Singh Khalra, before his assassination by the Punjab Police, had uncovered evidence to support the murder of tens-of-thousands of Sikhs by the Punjab Police.

The attack on the Sikh people was premeditated and carried out over several years until, eventually, the Indian Government declared a civil war. Before the Indian Government unleashed hell in 1984, they had planned for a civil war years prior. The Indian Government actually took the time and resources to build a life size replica of the Golden Temple Complex, in which the military rehearsed the attack. However, the story India sells is that the attack on the Complex wasn't much planned but more of a spontaneous act to capture "terrorists". Unfortunately, by constructing a replica and taking the time to work with foreign governments, the Indian Government demonstrated that they were planning for some time to attack the Complex and the Sikh culture with heavy artillery and soldiers.

The Sikhs eventually learnt of the planned attack. Through public speeches made by individuals such as Jarnail Singh, the Sikhs warned the Indian Government that if they attacked the Complex, the Sikh nation would defend itself. The individuals who were the supposed terrorists within the Complex were there to defend the Golden Temple. A General within the Indian army defected, Shahbeg Singh, one of the greatest Indian military minds of the 20th century, and he was instrumental in defending the Golden Temple Complex.

In retaliation for the honourless attack on the Golden Temple, the murder of the innocent, and the destruction of Sikh literature, two Sikhs murdered the Prime Minister of India, Indira Gandhi. After the murder of the Prime Minister, leading politicians of the Congress Party used the incident to further their agenda of terror and intimidation. They organized the 1984 anti-Sikh terror campaign.[7] Using voter lists, they systematically attacked Sikh households and businesses.[8] It's estimated that 10, 000 Sikhs were massacred during the anti-Sikh terror campaign.[9]

> *"For three days, gangs of arsonists and killers, in criminal collusion with the police and Congress politicians, who pointed out the houses of Sikhs, were allowed to rampage freely...No one was ever brought to trial."*[10]

> *"By all responsible accounts the government calmly stood by even when several of its functionaries led the killing mobs on the streets."*[11]

> *"The government controlled television Doordarshan, and the All India Radio began broadcasting provocative slogans seeking bloody vengeance, 'khoon ka badla khoon se lenge (Blood for blood!)'. Murderous gangs of 200 or 300 people led by the leaders, with policemen looking on, began to swarm into Sikh houses, hacking the occupants to pieces, chopping off the heads of children, raping women, tying Sikh men to tires set aflame with kerosene, burning down the houses and shops after ransacking them. Mobs stopped buses and trains, in and out of Delhi, pulling out Sikh passengers to be lynched to death or doused with kerosene and burnt alive."*[12]

During the riots, the government even went to the extent of exploiting the power of Bollywood to encourage the public to riot against the Sikhs. According to the documentary produced by Karnail Singh Peer Mohammad,

1984: a state-sponsored Sikh massacre, Amitabh Bachchan, through a televised message, is alleged to have provoked the public to riot and attack the Sikhs. It's claimed that he perpetuated the slogan, *"the bloodstains must reach the houses of those who killed Indira"*.[13] (Referring to all Sikhs).

Although the anti-Sikh campaign ended within a few days, state sponsored terrorism didn't. The campaign of terror and intimidation continued. Firstly, The Indian Government continued to label baptized Sikhs terrorists, although they were the group repeatedly attacked. Then they used those sorts of operational-terms to justify setting aside the civil liberties of Punjab for near a decade,[14] and to use 500, 000 Indian troops to violently occupy Punjab. The deaths of 250, 000 Sikhs was the result.[15] During this time period, from the year 1984 to approximately 1992, the Indian military targeted and killed anyone they wished, including innocent women and children.[16]

To that effect, special police units were established to terrorize the civilians.[17] Abduction squads were created to target the young and the strong baptized Sikh men, regardless if they were politically involved or not.[18] Punjab Police illegally held, tortured, and/or murdered[19] any Sikh who they thought was forwarding the idea of Sikh autonomy to cure the poor conditions of Punjab. Thousands upon thousands were secretly executed and secretly cremated by them.[20] And military and police units regularly burglarized Sikh households. They would accuse Sikh families of harbouring a terrorist. They would then force them out of their homes under the pretext of searching for that terrorist. Then they would rob the family of their valuables.

The case has also been made that the Indian Government committed acts of terror, through their agents, and then attributed those acts to the Sikhs so to provide some sort of evidence that the Sikhs were engaged in terrorist acts, and not acting in self-defence. It's an old trick used by many past and present governments, and the Indian Government is well known for their honourless tactics. They readily *"destabilize minority populations, provoke them into violence and then crack down on them."*[21]

But even more detrimental to the Sikh nation than the murder of the masses, during the violent occupation of Punjab, the Indian Government filtered the messages the media delivered to the Indian people and the international community. Domestically and on the world scene, the Sikhs were falsely depicted as the troublemakers and the Indian Government showcased itself as the victims of senseless Sikh violence. Before, during, and after the violent occupation of Punjab by the Indian Government, the Indian Government engaged in a disinformation campaign that falsely characterized the Sikhs as the terrorists. Sadly, the consequences of their disinformation campaign are yet to wash away.

In places the Sikhs had immigrated to such as Canada, the Sikhs did attempt to organize and bring attention to the plight of the Sikh people living in Punjab. Unfortunately, the Indian Government was much more cunning than the Sikhs were and the Indian Government readily planted pretenders amongst the Sikhs so to disrupt their work. They also bribed the Sikh leadership, those they could, to mislead and corrupt their people. Canadian law enforcement officers and agencies discovered that several Sikhs were paid by the Indian Government to monitor other Sikhs, and certain Punjabi newspapers in Canada were bought-off by the Indian Government. They were purposely publishing disinformation and depicting the Sikhs as the hooligans. Concurrently, they were not reporting or spinning the atrocities committed by the Indian Government.[22]

When the Sikhs in places such as Canada did manage to publicly protest against the inhuman behaviour of the Indian Government, the Indian Government would again outwit the Sikhs. They would sponsor counter-demonstrations designed to instigate violence and muddy the message the demonstrators were attempting to communicate.[23]

There is no question that the Indian Government attacked the Sikh nation on multiple fronts. There is no question that the Indian Government murdered innocent men, women, and children during their violent campaigns of terror and intimidation. There is no question that they attempted to neutralize the power base of a potential Sikh revolution by targeting young men. And there is no question that they manipulated the media to add muscle to their terrorist acts by depicting the oppressed as the villains. Unless of course, the quarter-million people they murdered were all terrorists.

If there were a quarter-million people, or even half of that number, willing to rebel to have their voices heard, that would indicate the state mechanisms designed to address the concerns of the people failed on a large scale.

Obviously, something wasn't right with the conditions the people existed in if such a large number of people were willing to oppose the state. In most cases, if the conditions of the state allow for the individual to acquire the basics free of any unreasonable restraints, and if an individual's social and safety needs are met, large numbers of people don't rebel against the state.

We must understand that people are hesitant to rebel, especially when the opponent is significantly more powerful as the Indian State was and is. In circumstances when the opponent is so powerful, confrontation isn't typically the first option. When a large number of people do rebel, all peaceful means must've been exhausted and the conditions must've continued to persist.

After the independence of India, the Indian Government attacked the Sikh nation in an attempt to reduce their collective power. Today, Punjab is in shambles. The cost of hardship and a government turned on its people have taken their toll. Poverty, depression, liquor, drugs, government corruption, and illiteracy are some of the ills that plague and the Sikh nation slowly falls.

Maybe, if the Indian Government didn't misuse and abuse the word "terrorist", the world could see the beauty in a rebuilt Sikh nation. Perhaps, if the world knew the truth, they would assist. Maybe, if the truth was popular, the international community would hold the Indian Government responsible for their domestic acts of terror.

It becomes more than evident, after reviewing the print news from the time period of the campaign of intimidation, that the Western reporters were tricked by the Indian Government. They were tricked to publicize misinformation and wrongly label the fighter of freedom a terrorist. And let's not forget that the British Government also participated in the honourless attack on the Sikh people, and I'm sure they too played their part in the international disinformation campaign.

The consequences of that campaign still haunt the Sikh people. Even still, there are instances when the Western media attempts to associate the word "terrorist" with those who fought to defend the Sikh people.

Appendix A Endnotes

1. Harnik Deol, <u>Religion and Nationalism in India: the case of the Punjab</u> (Routledge: London, 2000), p. 107.

2. Ibid., p. 108.

3. Martha Crenshaw, <u>Terrorism in Context</u> (Penn State Press: Pennsylvania, 1995), p. 385.

4. Amrik Singh and Ram Narayan Kumar, <u>Reduced to Ashes: The Insurgency and Human Rights in Punjab</u> (South Asia Forum for Human Rights: Nepal, 2003), p. 38.

5. Ibid.

6. Veena Das, <u>Life and Words: violence and the descent into the ordinary</u> (University of California Press: California, 2007), p. 130.

7. Harnik Deol, <u>Religion and Nationalism in India: the case of the Punjab</u> (Routledge: London, 2000), p. 109.

8. Om Gupta, <u>Encyclopedia of India, Pakistan and Bangladesh</u> (Isha Books: India, 2006), p. 131.

9. Harnik Deol, <u>Religion and Nationalism in India: the case of the Punjab</u> (Routledge: London, 2000), p. 109.

10. Thomas R. Metcalf, <u>A Concise History of Modern India</u> (Cambridge University Press: United States, 2006), p. 259.

11. P Lalan Tiwari, <u>Issues in Indian Politics</u> (Mittal Publications: New Delhi, India, 1995), p. 276.

12. Amrik Singh and Ram Narayan Kumar, <u>Reduced to Ashes: The Insurgency and Human Rights in Punjab</u> (South Asia Forum for Human Rights: Nepal, 2003), p. 42-43.

13. Sikhs for Justice: A Human Rights Advocacy Group. [http://www.sikhsforjustice.org/?q=content/amitabh-bachchan], January 2010.

14. Gerald James Jarson, <u>India's Agony over Religion</u> (SUNY Press: United States, 1995), p. 240.

15. Gus Martin, <u>Understanding Terrorism: Challenges, Perspectives, and Issues</u> (Sage Publications: United States, 2009), p. 190.

16. Martha Crenshaw, <u>Terrorism in Context</u> (Penn State Press: Pennsylvania, 1995), p. 396.

17. Jeffrey A. Sluka, <u>Death Squad: the anthropology of state terror</u> (University of Pennsylvania Press: Philadelphia, Pennsylvania, 2000), p. 209-210.

18. Ibid., p. 212-214.

19. Ibid., p. 220--222.

20. Amrik Singh and Ram Narayan Kumar, <u>Reduced to Ashes: The Insurgency and Human Rights in Punjab</u> (South Asia Forum for Human Rights: Nepal, 2003), p. 28-29.

21. Brian McAndrew and Zuhair Kasmeri, <u>Soft Target: the real story behind the Air India disaster</u> (James Lorimer &Company Ltd, Toronto, 2005), p. 35.

22. Ibid., p. 31.

23. Ibid.

Glossary

Age of Iron

The term "Age of Iron" refers to the fourth age in a series of four. Ancient Indian philosophy suggests that humanity continuously cycles through four ages.

According to the idea, the Age of Iron is the age contemporary humanity is in, and this age is said to be the darkest of all four. It is also the era furthest from the age of perfect existence.

The Age of Iron is considered home to untruths, and to one degree or another, almost all institutions are suggested to be infected by falsehoods. That includes the culture and the intelligence filled and shaped by those institutions.

The four ages are: The Golden Age of Sat Yuga, the Silver Age of Trayta Yuga, the Brass Age of Dwaapar Yuga, and the Iron Age of Kali Yuga.

Ahistorical

1. *"Unconcerned with or unrelated to (actual) history, historical development, or tradition."*
[http://www.thefreedictionary.com/ahistorical]

2. Constructed untruths presented as truths.

3. Recorded history that is incomplete or completely inaccurate but presented as a complete truth. There are two histories, one that is the truth and one that is created and presented as the truth. The second is typically created to serve the purposes of those able to propagate untruth.

Apocalypse

"Apocalypse, in the terminology of early Jewish and Christian literature, is a revelation of hidden things revealed by God to a chosen prophet or apostle. The term is often used to describe the written account of such a revelation. Apocalyptic literature is of considerable importance in the history of the Judeo-Christian-Islamic beliefs and traditions, because it makes specific references to beliefs such as the resurrection of the dead, judgment day, eternal life, final judgment and perdition."
[http://en.wikipedia.org/wiki/Apocalypse#Armageddon]

273

Aura

Aura refers to the quality, attitude, mood or feel of Thought Energy when secular, introspective, curious or intentional. Examples are mild happiness, moderate sadness, and extreme aggression. The two types of units that constitute the units of Aura are the units of emotion and the unit of energy/drive. Energy determines if the Aura is mild, moderate, or extreme.

a) Unit of Energy/Drive: The unit of energy motivates and produces the level of vigor.

b) Units of Emotion: The units of emotions produce feelings and create Thought Energy's Aura. For the most part, most people can identify what an emotion is, and most will agree that the human condition's emotions fall under two headings: positive and negative (with no relation to the ideas of good and evil).

Value configurations can evolve to mediate the units of emotion, and unlike the other innate units, the units of emotion do not activate when they lack information. On the contrary, they communicate only after stimulation. The type of emotion activated through stimulation is determined by the type of response a value configuration has towards information absorbed, accessed, or created.

Banda Singh (1670--1716)

Named by Guru Gobind Singh Ji, Banda Singh Bahadur is responsible for laying the secular foundation for what eventually became the Sikh Empire. In his fight against the tyrants, he organized the people of Punjab and brought the Mughals to their knees.

Caligula (12--41)

"The contemporaneous sources, Philo of Alexandria and Seneca the Younger, describe an insane Emperor who was self-absorbed, angry, killed on a whim, and who indulged in too much spending and sex. He is accused of sleeping with other men's wives and bragging about it, killing for mere amusement... causing starvation, and wanting a statue of himself erected in the Temple of Jerusalem for his worship."
[http://en.wikipedia.org/wiki/Caligula]

Collective Cognitive Condition

The collective cognitive condition, also known as "the angelic" and "the beautiful cognitive condition", develops, houses, nurtures, and reinforces a value system constituted by such beliefs and wants as contentment, compassion, truth, unconditional love, humility, virtue, righteousness, empathy, self-actualization, a transitive conscious condition, rationality, emotional stability, a desire for knowledge, the soul ("The Light within), a spiritual life purpose (a life purpose before and beyond a secular purpose), a sense of oneness with humanity, and a collective ego.

Collective Intelligence

The collective intelligence is constituted by the ideas, beliefs, wants, and knowledge most people have in common. The collective intelligence is typically transferred generation to generation; changing to reflect the changes that occur within the information popular culture communicates.

Darwinized

When I use the word "darwinized", I refer to the illusion of Darwin's Theory, the popular purposes given life by Darwinistic thought, and the ugly half of the mind's duality the theory has matured to nurture.

Decoded units of information

Decoded information is the product of the information absorbed through the senses. External information (primary information) is absorbed by the senses and converted into a format that the mind and Thought Energy can manipulate. All external information gathered is decoded and potentially encoded.

Deep Singh (January 26, 1682--November 13, 1757)

Deep Singh, along with Mani Singh, helped prepare the final text of *Guru Granth Sahib Ji*. However, that isn't the achievement that most remember Deep Singh for. Most remember Deep Singh as the brave and superhuman Singh who defeated the Afghan invaders to retake Amritsar--while holding his head from separating from his body.

In the year 1757, Ahmad Shah Abdali invaded India for the fourth time. On his return home, he was constantly harassed by the Sikhs. In retaliation, Ahmad Shah Abdali ordered the Sikh city of Amritsar be plundered, and the

Sikh sacred buildings in that city to be destroyed. After hearing of the tragedy, Deep Singh and a band of Sikhs vowed to retake the city.

During their march towards the city, they battled many Afghan soldiers. During one battle, Deep Singh received a blow to the neck that virtually severed his head from his body. But miraculously, and on hearing the cries of the Sikhs who followed him into battle, Deep Singh managed to hold his head in place with his left hand while he battled his way through the Afghan soldiers with a sword in the other. He eventually fell, but not before defeating the Afghans and reaching Amritsar.

Gordon Gekko
An immoral character played by Michael Douglas in the 1984 movie, *Wallstreet*, directed by Oliver Stone.

Guru Arjan (Sunday, May 2nd, 1563--Monday, June 16th, 1606)
Guru Arjan was the fifth of the ten living Gurus of Sikhie. He became Guru on Sept.16, 1581.

Guru Gobind Singh (Friday, January 5, 1666--Thursday, October 21, 1708)
"...was born 'Gobind Rai' and was the tenth and last of the ten human form Gurus of Sikhie. He became Guru on November 24, 1675, at the age of nine..."

"If we consider the work which (Guru) Gobind (Singh) accomplished, both in reforming his religion and instituting a new code of law for his followers, his personal bravery under all circumstances; his persevering endurance amidst difficulties, which would have disheartened others and overwhelmed them in inextricable distress, and lastly his final victory over his powerful enemies by the very men who had previously forsaken him, we need not be surprised that the Sikhs venerate his memory. He was undoubtedly a great man. (W, L. McGregor)"
[http://www.sikhiwiki.org/index.php/Guru_Gobind_Singh]

Guru Tegh Bahadur (Wednesday, April 18, 1621--Wednesday, November 24, 1675)
"...was the ninth of the Ten Gurus of Sikhie, becoming Guru on Saturday, April 16, 1664, following in the footsteps of his grand-nephew, Guru Har Krishan."
[http://www.sikhiwiki.org/index.php/Guru_Tegh_Bahadur]

Hari Singh (1791--1837)
In military prowess, the Great Hari Singh Nalwa has been compared to Napoleon, and that for conquering the likes of the Afghans. The Afghans still tell stories of the Great Hari Singh.

As a man of strength, Hari Singh has been compared to King Nall, the king who hunted lions and other beasts with his bare hands. But don't be mistaken, Hari Singh also had many saintly qualities.

Innate Wants
The innate units that create the innate wants are the unit of breathing, the unit of appetite, the unit of thirst, the unit of regulation, the unit of survival (including the avoidance of pain and programming such as the fight or flight reaction), and the unit of procreation.

Excluding the last, the innate wants are required for the human condition to exist, and excluding the unit of survival, these units are initially stimulated when there is a lack of information or too much.

Furthermore, each is eventually mediated by a value configuration (belief). After a value configuration is constructed, the value configuration gains the potential to activate the innate unit it was designed to mediate. However, this doesn't mean the innate unit loses the ability to activate when it requires information or when it's threatened.

The unit of procreation is a unit that influences a person to want to procreate. The unit of procreation isn't a unit designed to ensure the existence of the human condition, but the existence of the human race.

Jassa Singh
Raised by Mata Sundri, the widow of Guru Gobind, Jassa was a man known by many names. Early on, the Sikhs gave him the name "Guru Ka Lal" (the beloved son of the Guru). After the Khalsa freed Lahore from the Muslims in 1761, the Khalsa honoured him with the title of "Sultan-ul-Qaum" (king of the people). And after a battle against the Afghans to free 2200 of the most beautiful women captured and enslaved by the Muslims, he was known as "Bandi Chhor" (the Delivered). All of the women were free to go back to where they were from.

Jassa Singh eventually grew to lead the Khalsa. His leadership was vital in defeating the Afghan invaders. Without him, India would've been lost to the Muslims.

Language of deliberate deception
The phrase refers to the art of presenting inaccurate or incomplete information as if that information were true or complete. The technique is typically used to persuade others of the importance of a certain viewpoint.

In addition, and when the art of deception is practiced, information will be presented in such a way that a person will believe they independently reached the intended justification or conclusion.

Liberation
Within the context of the article, *Stepping Stone*, the word "liberation" represents the escape from the cycle of life and death.

Maya
"In the sacred writings of the Sikhs, this word has two meanings – one is mammon, as the word is here translated; the other is illusion or God's mystic power by which He created matter."
[Max Arthur Macauliffe, The Sikh Religion, Volume 1 (Forgotten Books, 2008), p. 68]

The term, Maya, represents the illusion that blinds the consciousness to the collective mind-independent reality and The Absolute. The collective mind-independent reality represents that which is natural. In addition to the built world, the collective mind-independent reality is also considered an agent of Maya, but unlike the world built by the human mind, the collective mind-independent reality is the playground through which The Absolute can be understood.

Memory
Memory is two-headed; it refers to the ability to recall and retain information, and it references the information retained.

278

All units of memory can be strengthened or weakened, in respect to their accessibility and longevity, and that can be done by nurturing the coding with the introduction of similar information.

Mencius (4th Century)

Mencius believed that benevolence and righteousness were innate attributes of a person. He also believed that sometimes human and worldly activities disguise those attributes.

Mencius used the Niu Mountain as an example to illustrate his point. The Niu Mountain was once beautiful; covered in an abundance of trees and vegetation. However, the local communities chopped down all the trees, and the local livestock trampled and grazed over the vegetation. As such, the mountain eventually lost its beauty.

When the local people would come across the mountain, they would only see the ugly the mountain had transformed to become. They had forgotten that it was once beautiful. They had forgotten that the mountain has regenerative powers. With a little rain and sunlight, how can the buds and sprouts not again appear?

The beauty of the mountain represents the good within the human condition, and sometimes, secular events can temporarily disguise that good. However, if that good is given attention and nourishment, by behaving good and absorbing information that reinforces the idea of good, it will again surface.

Miri Piri

"Miri--The word miri has been derived from the Persian word 'miri'...which literary means commander, governor, lord, prince, etc, and signifies temporal power. Piri--The word piri has been derived from the Persian 'pir' literary meaning senior man, saint, holy man, spiritual guide, head of a religious order, and stands for spiritual authority."
[http://www.sikhiwiki.org/index.php/Miri_and_Piri]

Naam

According to the Sikh philosophy, Naam is the divine light or creative energy present within the Universe and within everything. In addition, Naam is a principle of nature accessible by those individuals who've developed a consciousness oriented to perceive Naam. Finally, the term is also used to refer to the name of God.

Nanak (Saturday, April 15, 1469--Monday, September 22, 1539)

Founder of the Sikh faith and formally known as Guru Nanak Dev Ji, he, like Jesus, was a holy man who preached the message of One God and One Humanity. What's more, Guru Nanak emphasized the importance of good thoughts and actions good, remembering that there is truth in all religion, remembering The One, and the potential of every person to develop an interactive relationship with The Divine.

Guru Nanak is said to have travelled the world and to places like Saudi Arabia, Africa, Tibet, Afghanistan, Iran, Iraq, Egypt, Brazil, and supposedly, North America.

Guru Nanak also travelled to Rome, among other places not mentioned, and met with the Pope of then. As confirmed by the Vatican. It is said he also spoke with Martin Luther before Luther began his movement.

Nanak was the first of the ten Gurus of Sikhie. His inner light was appointed to the second Guru by him before his natural passing. That tradition continued until the Tenth Guru appointed the light to a collection of holy literature known as *Guru Granth Sahib Ji.*

Order of the Solar Temple

"In October 1994 Tony Dutoit's infant son (Emmanuel Dutoit), aged three months, was killed at the group's centre in Morin Heights, Quebec. The baby had been stabbed repeatedly with a wooden stake. It is believed that Di Mambro (group leader) ordered the murder because he identified the baby as the Anti-Christ described in the Bible. He believed that the Anti-Christ was born into the order to prevent Di Mambro from succeeding in his spiritual aim.

A few days later, Di Mambro and twelve followers performed a ritual Last Supper. A few days after that, apparent mass suicides and murders were conducted at two villages in Switzerland, and at Morin Heights."
[http://en.wikipedia.org/wiki/Order_of_the_Solar_Temple#Mass_murders_and _suicides]

Self-Actualization

"...the final level of psychological development that can be achieved when all basic and meta needs are fulfilled and the 'actualization' of the full personal potential takes place."
[http://en.wikipedia.org/wiki/Self_actualization]

Selfish Cognitive Condition

The dominant characteristics of a selfish cognitive condition are what trap a person's value system to the term "underdeveloped". The dominant characteristics of the selfish are beliefs that:

1) Suppress, weaken, contradict, or disguise the elements of the beautiful half.
2) Nurture only sensual fulfilment, a selfish existence, sensory satisfaction, individuality, and self interest.
3) Separate the self from humanity, communities, other people, The Absolute, the spirit, the Universe, and the planet.
4) Detail the individual with a higher value than humanity, other people, communities, death, The Absolute, the spirit, the Universe, and the planet.
5) Develop and nurture the selfish ego and the destructive elements that predominantly comprise the selfish ego.

Sinful Motion

A sinful motion is one that influences the self or another person to detach from the beautiful half of the mind's duality. When a person hurts another, not only do they detach from the beautiful, they also provoke the person they hurt to detach from the beautiful.

Social contract

"Social Contract Theory, nearly as old as philosophy itself, is the view that persons' moral and/or political obligations are dependent upon a contract or agreement between them to form society."
[http://www.iep.utm.edu/s/soc-cont.htm]

The Absolute

That which is truer than the collective mind-independent reality.

281

The built world

The term symbolizes the neo-liberal/neo-conservative system of consumption, wealth extraction, resource extraction, production, and distribution. The term also encompasses the popular culture and the collective intelligence that evolved to accommodate that ideology. The term "built world" does not encompass the natural world.

The machine

A term that symbolizes the neo-liberal/neo-conservative system of consumption, wealth extraction, resource extraction, production, and distribution. The term also encompasses the cultural and political atmosphere created to accommodate that ideology.

Third party comments

The term "third party comments" refers to a simple technique used to persuade a person of a particular viewpoint. The technique involves other people talking about the viewpoint you wish to sell to the masses in a positive manner.

This technique is often used within movies. For example, to create a reputation and to develop how the audience will perceive a character, the writer of the movie will script the other characters in the movie to comment on the perception the writer wishes to build. If the writer wanted the audience to think that the main character of the story is a gifted guitarist, the writer will have the other characters make comments pertaining to that talent. Maybe, they'll talk about the different awards he's won or at what age he first picked up a guitar. The same can be done if attempting to depict an idea.

Third party examples

Examples of the idea you wish to instil. If you would like people to interact a certain way when in a certain situation, give examples of people behaving in the manner you wish to instil. Moreover, create a positive aura to compliment the example.

Units of Manipulation

The units of manipulation are the units that enable, influence, frame and guide the information absorbed and manipulated within the mind. The units of manipulation are the five units of sense, the unit of Thought Energy, and the functional units. These units are determined to function a specific way.

a) The Five Units of Sense: The five senses create the sensations of touch, taste, smell, sight, and sound. They are the tools through which the person interacts with the environment, and each mind is home to senses that can function different from another's.

The five senses are with innate software that interprets the body's five senses and communicates the information gathered to the other agents of the mind.

b) The Unit of Thought Energy: A guest of the mind, Thought Energy can be in one of two fundamental conditions: awake or not. When awake, Thought Energy can be in one or more of five states: introspective, secular, intentional, curious, and uninhibited. Except when Thought Energy is uninhibited, Thought Energy can be in more than one state at once. The five states are:

i) Introspective--Pure introspection involves only internal information communicating to or accessed by Thought Energy. Furthermore, no primary information decoded (information absorbed from outside the human condition) is influencing the mapping of motions. In this state, Thought Energy is only manipulating information already within the metaphysical condition.

When introspective, Thought Energy is with a transitive consciousness: transitive lower order thought and/or higher order thought. Lower order thought refers to an individual thinking about the information communicated or accessed-- an individual is aware of the information in motion, including the Aura. Higher order thought involves the individual exercising her ability to manipulate that information to produce desired results.

ii) Secular--Pure secularism involves only primary information (external information) stimulating value configurations, and those configurations then influence the mapping of motions, and so on.

In a pure secular state, one is not introspective.

iii) Intentional--With propositional content, e.g., when Thought Energy is wanting or fearing. Furthermore, value configurations are the only able to stimulate the intentional state. In essence, a value configuration communicates the propositional content.

iv) Curious--An explorative and curious state.

v) Uninhibited--Within this state, Thought Energy is without introspection, secularism, curiosity, or intention. What's more, the time and space within the Thought Energy is empty, including the influence of any emotion.

Excluding the last, all states are stimulated, and each person is predisposed to a state that is more active than another's predispositions. In addition, the various states are eventually mediated by constructed value configurations, and the various states can be conditioned to activate more or less.

c) The Functional Units: The functional units of the mind enable the person to reason, to retain information, to recall information, to associate information, to label information, to categorize information, to build information, and to mimic information. They are the abilities of the mind. Eventually, each is mediated by a value configuration--a belief about the functional unit. That belief activates every time the functional unit is used or accessed.

Each mind is home to units that can function at different levels. For example, one mind might be able to reason more conclusively than another might, another mind might be able to make associations faster, and another mind might be able to remember in more detail.

Unit of thought

Simply put, any thought is a unit of thought. If a thought is encoded, it becomes a unit of memory.

The Changing Of Guard

With my feet up and a cold drink, it doesn't feel all that wrong to watch the changing of guard, and it doesn't feel all that wrong to gaze at the stars.

I've been blessed in the sense that I didn't grow in an American ghetto, on a Canadian reservation, or in the middle-ages. There are no gunshots to waste thought on. There are no extremely poor socio conditions that limit the parameters my thoughts are created within. And modern times prescribe no fall harvest to wake early for. Peace in mind has freed my time to watch the stars slowly compose themselves, slowly reveal themselves, and slowly share the stories only they can tell.

Last year, star gazing, they told the story of evil and good. They awoke an Eastern thinker who hugged me with his words and revealed the world behind the world. Mystically, inducing the truth above them both; describing hell as mortal and heaven on earth--describing both as principles of the Universe.

This past month we went back to the Big Bang and they showed how they and "I" were distant family. After which, they took the time to help me understand the "I" in me and to showed how the "I" is actually three: chemistry, surroundings, and energy.

Two nights ago, they extended their hands and pulled me up to sit with them. Through the eyes of a star, Muslims, Christians, and Hebrews prayed together in Jerusalem. We must've time traveled. And although there were brief periods in time when they all sat together, I'm hoping at tomorrow we marvelled.

And last night I saw the most incredible. I saw harmony on earth, a peaceful transformation of those who destroy her, a culture of the Philosopher King and the Holy-Trooper, a people who love The One Eternal Creator, and benevolent eco-political leaders.

Incredibly, just stars to some. Just twinkles of dust on a black canvas. But to men and women like me, they are gateways to the imagination and the heart. To men and women like me, they are the stuff worthy of thought. With my feet up and a cold drink, it doesn't feel all that wrong to watch the changing of guard, and it doesn't feel all that wrong to gaze at the stars.

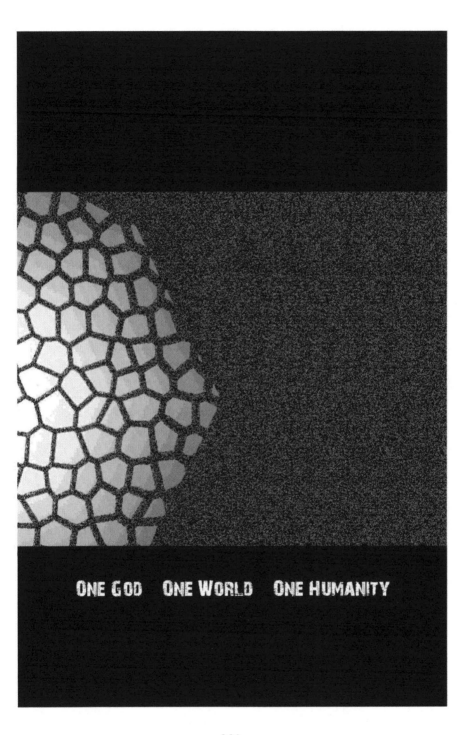

ONE GOD   ONE WORLD   ONE HUMANITY

Made in the USA
Charleston, SC
23 March 2016